A Practical Guide to
Teaching and Learning

A Practical Guide to Teaching and Learning

Oran Tkatchov and
Shelly Kraynak Pollnow

ROWMAN & LITTLEFIELD EDUCATION

A division of

ROWMAN & LITTLEFIELD PUBLISHERS, INC.

Lanham • New York • Toronto • Plymouth, UK

Published by Rowman & Littlefield Education
A division of Rowman & Littlefield Publishers, Inc.
A wholly owned subsidary of The Rowman & Littlefield Publishing Group, Inc.
4501 Forbes Boulevard, Suite 200, Lanham, Maryland 20706
http://www.rowmaneducation.com

Estover Road, Plymouth PL6 7PY, United Kingdom

British Library Cataloguing in Publication Information Available

Library of Congress Cataloging-in-Publication Data

Tkatchov, Oran.
    A practical guide to teaching and learning / Oran Tkatchov and Michele Pollnow.
        p. cm.
    Includes bibliographical references.
    ISBN 978-1-61048-071-0 (cloth : alk. paper)—ISBN 978-1-61048-072-7 (pbk. : alk.
paper)—ISBN 978-1-61048-073-4 (electronic)
    1. Effective teaching.   2. Learning.   I. Pollnow, Shelly.   II. Title.
    LB1025.3.T58 2011
    371.102—dc23   2011034889

∞™ The paper used in this publication meets the minimum requirements of American National Standard for Information Sciences—Permanence of Paper for Printed Library Materials, ANSI/NISO Z39.48-1992.

Printed in the United States of America

Contents

Acknowledgments

The authors would like to thank the following: Past and present coworkers, Alex, Luba, Tya, Diane, Kristen, and the rest of the Tkatchov/Korostil family, Dave and Meagan Pollnow, John and Mary Louise Kraynak and family, Geri and Jim Borgen, Amanda Pfau, Anita Archer, Cheryl Lebo, and Phyllis Schwartz.

Introduction

A Practical Guide to Teaching and Learning contains a compilation of 15 main ideas or concepts that will help teachers to become better at what they do to help learners reach their potential. Each concept is a common sense approach that is backed by research and provides an understanding of what a teacher should know and be able to do as an effective professional in his/her classroom. Ultimately, it is the teacher behaviors that have an impact on the student behaviors, and each chapter provides sound suggestions and tips to set the teaching and learning relationship up for success.

At the end of the chapters, there are Reflection Scenarios to assist the reader in thinking through possible issues and assist the reader in applying the concept to situations in his/her own practice. There are also guiding questions to stimulate personal reflection and to facilitate conversation if using the book for a book study for professional learning community dialog and discussion.

The early chapters are introduced as a guide to help teachers set up their classrooms at the beginning of the school year. Teachers should find Chapters 1–5 particularly helpful in coming to a common understanding of effective classroom management, culture and climate as well as tips for involving families, a guaranteed and viable standards-based curriculum, differentiated and tiered instruction, balanced assessment systems, and attendance and student motivation.

The middle Chapters, 6–13, focus on improving instruction for all students. The authors provide current research on promising best practices from well-known experts in the field. The importance of student engagement in terms of meaningful participation is explained with many strategies for teachers to apply and practice. Multiple intelligences are described with many techniques and approaches cited to match learning styles of diverse populations of students.

A chapter is devoted to the importance of background knowledge in the teaching and learning process. Examples and strategies are given to address the need for providing background knowledge as a scaffold to level the academic playing field for all students no matter their family circumstances and position in life. This idea of background knowledge forms a foundation for the next chapter on vocabulary and the explicit instruction methods necessary to close the achievement gap as quickly possible for our struggling readers.

There is an easy-to-understand chapter on Response to Intervention (RTI) that is the process that is often employed with struggling readers and math students. The authors seek to help the reader to understand the process and the vital component of core reading and math programs that need to be in place before any other interventions are implemented.

In the chapter on coaching, the authors make the link between effective implementation of programs in reading or any other content area. The presence of good instructional and content coaches is seen as a necessary component in any professional development model. According to current research, coaching ups the implementation of new strategies in the classroom significantly and improves the teaching and learning process.

Chapter 13 outlines specific strategies to improve teaching and learning of writing skills. The authors have included a chapter on writing to satisfy many of their colleagues' requests for more writing strategies.

Finally, the last two chapters are all about the teacher's learning. These chapters contain the most current research on effective professional development that leads to deep knowing and understanding. As the professional develops into an educational leader, there are opportunities to share learning with others, and the final chapter briefly describes some ways to effectively share knowledge with peers. The authors hope this easy-to-read, thin, little book is a quick reference that you keep in the top drawer of your teacher's desk (what we teachers often refer to as our "belly" drawer) and that it helps to set the stage for success in your day-to-day business of teaching and learning.

Chapter 1

Quality Classroom Leaders and Setting the Stage for a Successful School Year

Exploring the old and deducing the new makes a teacher.

—Confucius

Ignorance is the curse of God; knowledge is the wing wherewith we fly to heaven.

—William Shakespeare

With all the computer-based programs, multi-tiered interventions, assessment software, aligned textbooks, and scripted curriculum available to the field, some might question if the role of the teacher is significant in today's schools. Does it really matter who is leading the classroom? The answer to this question is a resounding *yes!*

Take a minute and think back to your favorite class. Chances are you don't remember the name of the textbook, the name of the computer software, or the order in which the curriculum was taught. What you do remember is the person in charge of that class: the teacher.

For Oran Tkatchov, one of this book's authors, it was Mrs. Baron and her creative writing class. He doesn't remember what period it was, or who sat behind him. He doesn't remember what literature was read, or even the color of the textbook. He does remember her making him feel like his work mattered and that he could do better. She showed genuine interest when he did a presentation on the punk-rock poet Henry Rollins and used that moment to convince him to write a paper comparing his anger to the rage in Maya Angelou's writing. Because of this, he had no problem learning about iambic

1

pentameter or actually reading Maya Angelou during his free time. This interest to read wasn't instilled by a video collection, a laptop computer, or comfortable classroom furniture; it came from a teacher who possessed the skills necessary to get him excited to learn.

Quality teaching is the key to student achievement. Although there are many new resources available to schools, research states that the individual teacher's skills are still important to student success. In order for students to learn, they must be able to do three things: access background knowledge, make connections, and put new understanding into context. The new learning needs to make sense based on the past information or background information the student already has about that topic. Students of teachers who can convey higher- and lower-order thinking skills regularly outperform students whose teachers only convey lower-order thinking skills (Langer and Applebee, 1987; Wenglinsky, 2000). For students to learn and actually want to learn, they must be faced with a challenge but also feel like they are *being supported* while facing that challenge. Other studies have come to the same conclusion: teacher quality appears to be more related to student success than class size and monetary spending (Darling-Hammond, 2000).

Recently, *The Los Angeles Times* used the value-added analysis to rate teachers based on student progress from year to year (Felch, Song, and Smith, 2010). Their data stated:

- Effective teachers constantly take students who perform below grade level and boost them to at or above grade level within one academic year.
- Some students get ineffective teachers for more than one year in a row.
- Effective and ineffective teachers are found in all schools, not just "rich" districts or "poor" districts.
- A parent's choice of a teacher can be more influential in a student's success than the choice of school. Per the findings, a teacher can have three times as much influence on a student's academic progress as the school they attend.
- A student's race, socio-economic background, previous achievement level or English proficiency does not play a major role in whether a teacher is effective or not.

Other researchers (Sanders and Rivers, 1996) concur with these findings and state that the teacher effect is "the most dominant factor affecting students' academic gain." How dominant of a factor? Let's put this into context: the same study found that students who spent three straight years with the most effective teachers had a 50-percentile point advantage over students who spent three straight years with the least effective teacher.

Another study found that in one school year, students taught by the top five percent of teachers were able to show 1.5 year's growth, while students taught by the lowest 5 percent of teachers showed only a one-half year's growth (Hanushek, 1971). Now let's remember that it is common for a student to have an ineffective teacher for more than one year in a row. Based on these studies, one can conclude that the influence of a good teacher can alone mean years of more growth to an individual child. On the same note, one can conclude that the influence of a bad teacher can mean years of growth that were not achieved. The most important resources in our schools are our teachers, and research shows that effective teachers using good instructional practices increase student academic achievement.

At this point, one could argue "Well that's probably true for any profession. Those who get the better employees get better service." This is correct, but in the field of education, we need *all* teachers to be exemplary because our final product is the future. A poorly made car, sofa, or meal can be easily discarded or junked. Poorly educated children cannot—they stick around and tend to hurt society. One study states that dropouts are almost four times more likely to be arrested than high school graduates and more than eight times as likely to be incarcerated. This should scare you. Sixty-eight percent of state prison inmates don't have a high school diploma (Dropouts and Crime, 2008). Can you imagine what the world would be like if even half of these folks were able to finish high school? We don't want to go on a rant here, but in a society where teachers tend to be the first to be blamed and the last to be paid, we as professionals need to remind ourselves why we put up with this: because we have a higher calling and we *know* we can be the change we want to see in the world.

Many studies over the last 15 years have researched the qualities of exemplary teachers. The personalities and appearances of quality teachers will vary: some seem traditional in look and speech, while others appear eccentric and over-the-top. Despite these differences, certain attributes of quality teachers remain consistent. Multiple sources suggest that exemplary teachers:

- possess a verbal adeptness to communicate to students,
- have a firm grasp of the content knowledge they teach,
- are life-long learners,
- use different instructional approaches to meet the needs of diverse learners,
- are certified by the state in which they teach, and
- have experience teaching.

Also found in exemplary teachers are:

- A continuous focus on student learning. Exemplary teachers know a good day is not based on whether the students obeyed their rules and listened but is based on what the students actually learned. The focus is on the student learning, not the teacher.
- A continuous study of student work. Exemplary teachers are always looking for evidence of what the student learned, as well as what *exactly* the student did not learn. These teachers are always looking at student work as a way to collect data and alter instruction.
- Continuous engagement of the students in learning. Exemplary teachers find ways to include problem solving and real-world applications in the instructional practice. Real-world applications tend to keep students interested by answering the question "Why do I need to know this?"
- Continuous study of the craft of teaching. Exemplary teachers are up-to-date on best practices regarding classroom instruction, brain-based research, and current theory. Kids are always changing, technology is always changing, and therefore the teaching profession will always have to adapt.
- Reflective practice. Exemplary teachers always look back on a lesson to analyze what went right and how it can be duplicated. Exemplary teachers always look back on a lesson to analyze what went wrong and how it can be improved.
- Goal setting. Exemplary teachers have a professional vision as to where they want to be, and also set reasonable yet rigorous goals for themselves and their class. As a young teacher, Oran was asked by his mentor "Where do you want to be in five years?" He hated the question, but looking back, it made him think about how he could advance as a teacher and ended up being useful as he always thought about his future learning.
- Model good teaching. Exemplary teachers model good teaching. It sounds silly, but most teachers *know* what good teaching is, but their classroom practice does not resemble what they know. Knowing it is easy; doing it is the part that takes practice. Good teachers bridge the knowing-doing gap.

It is no longer a guessing game as to what qualities are found in effective teachers; we know what needs to take place in a classroom to maximize time and increase student success. Why doesn't it happen? Some teachers have had bad examples of what teaching should look like. Many teachers exhibit the teaching behaviors they saw when they were students or those imparted by their master teacher during the student teaching practicum. Some teachers replicate what they see other teachers doing in their school without knowing if what they are replicating is good practice. Some teachers are just burnt out and are buying time before they can retire.

The authors of this book have noticed that most teachers fall into bad habits even though they have the best intentions. Once teachers get into the flow of teaching, they tend to get comfortable, even if they aren't getting the wanted results. It's no different than trying to change your golf swing or eating habits. By no means is it easy, but with time, coaching, and consistency, the implementation of best practices and a handful of good instructional strategies will set the foundation for a successful and rewarding career in education.

Effective teachers need to have the commitment to model what is expected from the students, and model what is known to be effective teaching at all times. There are no shortcuts. We must commit to being committed. We must wake up knowing we can and will do what's necessary to change a student's life for the better.

Now the authors of this book aren't fortune tellers, but we can tell you either what happened during your first year of teaching or predict what will happen to you during the first year of teaching. How? Research, my dear Watson! In general, there are five phases that new teachers go through (Moir, 1999).

The first phase of first-year teaching is the *anticipation phase*. During this phase, teachers cannot wait to change the world and impart wisdom throughout the class. Scenes from movies like *Stand and Deliver* or *The Great Debaters* run through their heads. They are excited and feel incredibly prepared from their pre-service to tackle the teaching job! The anticipation phase usually lasts for a few weeks.

The next phase is called the *survival phase*. Within a month, teachers feel overwhelmed. Things are happening fast, and situations occur that were never taught in college. It seems like there's never enough time to catch up on grading, and self-reflection is difficult because teachers are just trying to not break down or break something. Lesson plans might not seem to work, although a ton of time was used to create the plan. Amazingly, though, this experience is what will help these teachers become better in the long term.

Following the survival phase is the *disillusionment phase*. After about two months of just surviving, new teachers tend to feel burned out, depressed, or even question if they chose the right profession. More work seems to be piled on as the first grading period ends, and parent conferences begin. It's been noted that around this time many new teachers start to take sick days more often. Sounds horrible, right? Well, just when things seem like they couldn't get worse . . . they don't! After this phase the frown turns itself upside down.

After being beaten down in the disillusionment phase, most teachers find a way to pull themselves up by their britches. The fourth phase is called the *rejuvenation phase*. This usually begins around the winter break, when teachers get some well-deserved rest and relaxation. Teachers have time to reflect on what they went through and how they can do a better job when they return after the break. At this point, the reality of this job really begins to soak in. This phase will usually get the teacher through the rest of the school year.

The last phase is the *reflection phase*, which begins around May. At this point, teachers look back at what worked and what didn't, and begin thinking about how they can make the next year so much better. Teachers go through their first year lesson plans and decide what to reuse and what to discard. If you are a new teacher, the authors hope that the content of this book will make your survival and disillusionment phases a little easier to handle.

CLASSROOM MANAGEMENT

Classroom management is the foundation for student achievement. It is the underpinning of effective teaching. If teachers cannot manage their classroom, they will not be able to teach. *You will not survive as a teacher if you don't have effective classroom management.* Most teachers who do not master classroom management leave the profession within the first five years of teaching.

Researcher Robert Marzano (Marzano and Pickering, 2003) observes "A classroom that is chaotic as a result of poor management not only doesn't enhance achievement, it might even inhibit it." Carolyn Evertson and Alene Harris (Evertson and Harris, 1995) state that "teachers whose students demonstrated high on-task rates and academic achievement implemented a systematic approach toward classroom management at the beginning of the school year."

Teachers must set the stage to allow for the deepest, most rigorous learning possible for each of their students. Consistent classroom procedures and the physical arrangement of the room play significant roles in establishing a learning environment that increases academic achievement, social growth, and instructional time.

Often times a new teacher will hear the old adage, "It is always easier to get nicer as the year goes on than to get tougher." This saying holds some truth, but a more appropriate saying is, "Your expectations and consequences need to be consistent from day one until the bell rings on the final day for the school year." *The truth of the matter is that if you let a student do something on the first day of school, expect them to continue doing it for the rest of the year.* Good classroom habits and manners are not a result of happenstance but are intentionally taught and reinforced throughout the year. This really is no different than raising a child or training a puppy. It is important to praise the actions we want to see more often, and it is important to assign consequences to the actions we want to limit.

The first thing a teacher needs to do is create the "non-negotiable" classroom rules and procedures, and enforce the rules and procedures consistently—every day for every student. Rules are different than procedures, but both are needed to create an orderly classroom. *Rules* are meant to guide behavior, whereas *procedures* deal with the day-to-day processes in the classroom. Just like a well-run household, the classroom needs to have rules and procedures. The rules in your class should help create an emotionally safe environment. A positive emotional classroom climate contains five aspects (Walker, 2004):

- Acceptance of the teacher. Students need to know that the teacher believes they can succeed.
- Acceptance by peers. Students need to know that they are part of a learning community and will not be hurt or put down. The sense of "belonging" in a school has many benefits, including reduced drop-out rates, fewer discipline issues, and increased academic success (Christle, Jolivette, and Nelson, 2007).
- A sense of order. Students need to know that there is a pattern to what the teacher is doing and that there is a routine within the class.
- Clarity of tasks. Students need to understand what they are expected to do.
- Resources for success. Students need to know that they have access to the tools needed for success.
- Emotional intelligence. Students need to know they can express emotion regarding the learning.

Teachers should have approximately seven rules for secondary classes and five to eight for elementary classes (Evertson, Emmer, and Worsham, 2003). Anything more than eight will be difficult for the students to remember and difficult for the teacher to remember. Although some rules are non-negotiable, most rules are more effective when students have input and take ownership. By more effective, we mean there's a better chance the students will obey the rules and not question why the rule is in place.

As previously stated, procedures are the day to day processes in the classroom. The number of procedures in a classroom should also be limited and should have a purpose. Procedures can include how to turn in homework, how to enter and leave the classroom, how to get materials, how to work in partners, or even how to use the restroom. Harry Wong offers "The Three-Step Approach to Teaching Classroom Procedures" to be taught at the beginning of every year (Wong, 1991):

Explain: State, explain, model, and demonstrate the procedure. Students need to know why the rule is in place and the purpose behind it. Don't assume the student knows how to adhere to the rule. Model what "whisper" should sound like. Model what an organized desk looks like. Although this may seem like a waste of time, pre-correcting any misunderstandings the first day will save you time as the school year progresses.

Rehearse: Rehearse and practice the procedure under your supervision. Make sure the students are capable of performing the procedure. Sometimes the classroom layout will prevent a student from seeing the board or talking quietly to a partner. Students with English as a second language or who are from another country might interpret the procedure to mean something different. By modeling and rehearsing, the teacher can ensure all students are "on the same page."

Reinforce: Re-teach, rehearse, practice, and reinforce the classroom procedure until it becomes a student habit or routine. Repeat this process as needed. Remember the old saying "If you expect it, then you must teach it." This is the most important step, especially in the beginning of the year. Applaud students for correctly following procedures (make them a positive example while providing positive reinforcement), and politely correct students who have yet to make it a routine.

Some students might test the teacher by diverging from classroom procedures. In these cases, politely and quietly remind the student of the procedure by comparing their behavior to the rules. Don't make it personal. Do not bring the attention of the class to the negative behavior. In time, the student will see that the teacher is not letting up and will adhere to the procedure. At this time, politely and quietly reinforce the positive behavior.

As the year progresses, consistently enforce the classroom procedures, which might mean the teacher stops to state, explain, model, and demonstrate the procedure again. This is important for all grades and age groups. Make sure that the classroom rules are posted in an area where they are observable to both the teacher and the students. To reiterate, *promote the positive examples, and quietly correct the negative examples.* Make it a standard routine to review, reinforce, and rehearse classroom procedures as new students join your classroom or after extended breaks and holidays.

The key to all this is no matter how much you have to remind the class of the routines and rules, enter the classroom everyday and treat your students like they have met your expectations. Don't go into it with the attitude that the class will once again be out of control. Keep your expectations high and believe that all students will meet these expectations.

As stated earlier, rules are more effective when students have input and take ownership. There's a good chance that the students will want what you want for rules. As a teacher, you can guide many of these student suggestions to get to what you want to see in the classroom. For instance, in an elementary school, a student might say "I don't want Jimmy touching my desk." As a teacher, you can reply, "Okay, so we want to keep our hands to ourselves? We can make that a rule."

After creating the rules and the routines, the teacher needs to think about the consequences for not adhering to the rules and routines. Similar to "The Three-Step Approach to Teaching Classroom Procedures," involving students to some extent in the process often creates buy-in and serves to help students take ownership of the procedures, rules, and consequences. Develop a step-by-step set of actions that will occur if rules and procedures are not followed, explain and model the actions to the students, post the set of actions in the classroom, and provide a copy to parents.

The following is an example from a 6th grade classroom as teacher and students develop rules and consequences:

> This was an inclusion classroom that had 34 students that included 2 special needs students, 9 students qualified as gifted, 7 students qualified for special education, 4 students identified as English Language Development, a paraprofessional for the special needs students, and a general education/gifted education teacher. Twelve of the students qualified for free and reduced lunch. The school did not have a school-wide discipline program, but there were school rules in place. The class began the process of developing rules and consequences for their classroom on the first day of school. The teacher set the stage by reminding the class they would probably be living and spending as much time together in their classroom during the school year as they spent at home with their families. Since it was quite likely that there would be times when all 36 people in the 20'×18' space would not all be having a good day, rules and consequences would have to be in place to guide our behavior and promote a safe and productive environment for their classroom. There were sheets of posters situated around the room. One poster listed the school rules with the consequences, and other posters listed non-negotiable classroom rules with consequences, as well as blank posters for "Additional Rules and Consequences" as a heading. Student teams rotated around the room discussing the rules, adding comments, and any additional rules and consequences that they thought might be necessary. The teacher guided the classroom discussion on what rules and consequences would be appropriate to make their classroom a place of safety, productivity, and respect for both students and teachers.

These consequences should be in accordance with the school's student handbook and must *never* humiliate or disrespect the student. Once upon a time, there was a stance that by embarrassing a student, the teacher was "teaching them a lesson," and this embarrassment would prevent the student from doing the action in question again. Let's make this clear: publicly embarrassing students won't make them better students. What it will do is make them despise school and despise you! It is not the cruelty of the consequence that will make a difference in your classroom, but the consistency in enforcing the rules that will.

When delivering a consequence, don't make it personal. Try to remain calm and unemotional, explain the inappropriate action, remind the student of the positive action you'd like to see, and then get back into the mode of teaching. Do not make the delivery of the consequence a huge, theatrical event.

Most important, listen to the student about why the behavior happened. As we know, actions that promote effective listening include:

• Attending fully with mind, body, and heart
• Listening with the intentions to understand what the speaker is trying to communicate
• Setting aside whatever may interfere with your focus on the speaker and the message
• Paying attention to the total message, both verbal and non-verbal
• Being empathetic to the feelings being expressed
• Refraining from judging the speaker, the communication style, or the message
• Being patient (Fitterer, Harwood, Locklear, Wright, Fleming, and Levinsohn, 2004)

Even thought the action of the child was not appropriate, it is important that the teacher hears from the student why the behavior happened and then provides a way to correct the behavior in the future. This cannot occur if the teacher does not listen to the student's explanation for the behavior.

The physical arrangement of the classroom is just as important as classroom procedures in creating a manageable classroom. Harry Wong predicts that the very first thing an effective teacher will ask of a student is for the student to find their assigned seat. *Do not let students pick where they want to sit!* Best practices state:

• Seating arrangements should support the purpose of the lesson format; therefore, it is important that the room configuration be flexible and changeable.
• Students who need more monitoring, the "high maintenance students," should be seated at the front of the class, or where the teacher can easily see them, as well as away from anything that can provide a distraction.

- Students should rehearse and practice a limited number of room configurations that will support a few basic learning structures just as students practice and rehearse procedures (Evertson and Harris, 1992).

  For example:

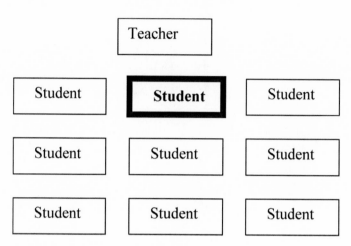

Figure 1.1   Classroom Style Seating

Classroom style seating is the traditional set up. This is good for lectures and test taking. The high maintenance student is in bold.

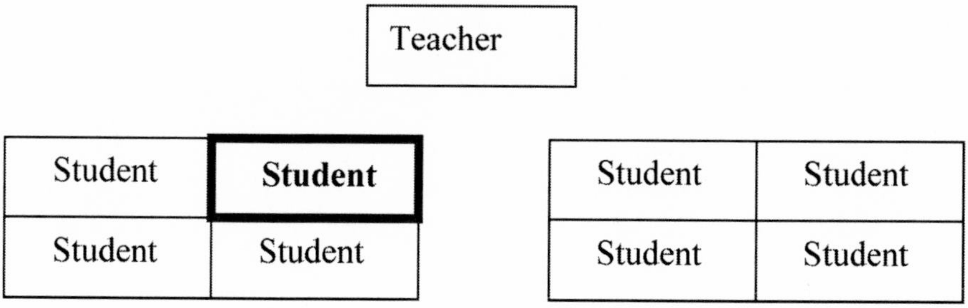

Teacher	

Student	**Student**		Student	Student
Student	Student		Student	Student

Figure 1.2   Pod Style Seating

Pod style seating works well when students are working in groups or centers. This provides the students a common work space.

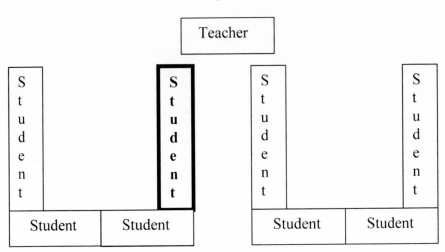

Figure 1.3 U-Shaped Seating

U-Shape seating works well when the students will be working with a partner as well as individually. This allows everyone the ability to listen to the teacher for direct instruction portions of the lesson.

The class seating chart should change throughout the semester, and the students should be aware that the seating chart will change often. In the beginning of the year, a seating chart will help the teacher remember the names of the students. The seating chart should be written down and used as a tool to take attendance. As personalities and student achievement becomes evident, the seating arrangement should maximize the effectiveness of the room. Partners for reading or math should be close to each other. Attention deficit students should remain close to the teacher and away from distractions. Some teachers, especially in elementary grades, will change the classroom configuration throughout the day.

Research (Jones, 2000) suggests using good masking tape to mark the position of the desks for the most often-used arrangement. This will help reduce time when returning to the standard arrangement and keep desks orderly when teaching middle and high school. Check with the school janitor to see if this is okay for the floors (if he says no, then ask the principal and explain why this will be beneficial to the class). It is important to be able to change the arrangement of the class with as little effort or distractions as necessary.

The physical arrangement of the classroom should allow the teacher to easily move throughout the classroom and have clear access to all students. The area where the teacher will be delivering the direct instruction portion of the lesson should provide visual clarity of all students. *If the classroom design does not allow for easy movement and clear vision, then the classroom must be redesigned.* Any bulletin boards, televisions, artifacts, computer screens, and so on need to be placed in areas of the room that do not block the teacher's vision of the classroom or block access of movement. Make sure all student materials (books, backpacks, etc.) are also placed in appropriate areas. These items should be placed where they cannot be a distraction to the students or where the teacher and students will stumble over them.

Not all kids will respond correctly even if you do everything to limit classroom disruptions with active engagement within lessons and excellent classroom routines. For those students who continue to test you as well as the classroom rules, other approaches might be needed.

Behavior plans are a good start, but only if they are approached correctly. With a behavior plan, the teacher, student, and preferably the student's parents agree to which positive behaviors will occur in the class and what negative behaviors will not occur within the class. This is written down and states what will occur if the student behaves in the positive manner as well as what will happen if the student behaves in the negative manner.

The crucial part of writing a behavior plan is that the teacher and the school need to provide the student with resources to succeed behaviorally. These behaviorally challenged students tend to not know how else to behave, so the school needs to explicitly provide the student with examples of how to act appropriately in specific situations. As the teacher, try to collect classroom data on when the child tends to misbehave, list when the outbursts tend to happen, and determine what triggers the misbehavior. Ask the student what tends to trigger the behavior and what events in the classroom make them respond inappropriately. Once these items are noted, come up with alternative behaviors the student can exhibit or, as a teacher, change the item if it is appropriate and will still work for the rest of the class. The key is to find out when the outbreaks occur and why the student reacts that way so the disruptive stimulus can be changed or the behavior to the stimulus altered.

Another great idea is to ask other teachers if they witness these behaviors and how they handle them. If other teachers do not see the poor behavior, ask what they are doing in their class during the times that the student acts inappropriately in your class. Try to give the student a predicable routine in the class. Try to provide the student more support and more structure. The support should be positive and praise good behavior as well as support the positive behavior by correcting negative behavior when it is present. As stated earlier when enforcing rules and procedures, all types of behavior supports should not be embarrassing or demeaning to the student.

An easy way to remember the key items discussed in this chapter for behavior is the acronym CHAMP, which is the framework that supports behavior (Sprick, Garrison, and Howard, 1998).

- Conversation—Are students seated where they can talk to each other if needed? What is the voice level for the activity?
- Help—What do you do when you need help?
- Activity—What is the activity you'll be teaching them? Will it be engaging? In future chapters we'll address the important topic of making sure your students are engaged.
- Movement—Can you move around the room safely? Can the students move around the room safely?
- Participation—How will you know if the students are participating? What does "participating" behavior look like? Do the classroom rules support this behavior?

The buzz overheard in the teachers' lounge for the current school year may be words like rigor, uncovering the content, background knowledge, differentiated instruction, and active engagement, but unless the learning setting is structured, all good intentions for success may be thwarted.

Rules, procedures, and a classroom set up to accommodate learning formats will help the teacher and students to maximize instructional time and foster success throughout the school year. The rules, procedures and classroom set-up allow the teacher to begin the actual art of teaching in an atmosphere that promotes a safe learning environment where teacher and students function as a productive and respectful team.

REFLECTION SCENARIO

Mr. R, a first year teacher at ABC High School, has had the same classroom instruction routine since he began teaching in August. It is now October and as students enter the room, he asks them to take a seat wherever they wish. He then takes attendance as students talk to their friends (it takes him 10 minutes since they are not in assigned seats, but he knows the class will be more enjoyable if the students get to sit with their friends. As soon as Mr. R finishes recording any absences he gathers his notes and begins lecturing for the next 45 minutes to his class of 30 students. The desks are askew in what at the beginning of the class were six neat rows. A few students take notes, but most continue talking. Mr. R asks the students "to keep it down," and keeps turning up the volume on his own voice as the lecture progresses talking over the chatter in the classroom. With five minutes to go, and Mr. R's voice just discernable above the din, Mr. R stops, asks if there are any questions, assigns homework and the bell rings. Mr. R teaches next door to your room and comes to you after school in desperation, truthfully describes his class, and asks for your help. How do you respond?

Chapter 2

What Are You Going to Teach Them?

Through learning we re-create ourselves. Through learning we become able to do something we were never able to do.

—Peter Senge

If the education of our kids comes from radio, television, newspapers—if that's where they get most of their knowledge from, and not from the schools—then the powers that be are definitely in charge, because they own all those outlets.

—Maynard James Keenan

Successful management is only one part of being a successful teacher. Knowing your content area (mathematics, English, social studies) is also important, but in this day and age of assessment and accountability, it is also important to know exactly *what* you are supposed to teach the students and *when* they are supposed to know it. This is called having a *guaranteed and viable curriculum*. What is a guaranteed and viable curriculum? A guaranteed and viable curriculum is a plan of what the teacher will teach and what the students will learn (Marzano and Pickering, 2003). The learning is based on an academic standard, can be taught in the time provided, and has explicit and specific objectives for every subject area, grade level, and course. Most states have state standards, and now with the creation of the Common Core Standards, many states will be teaching the same standards nationwide. These standards, in collaboration with text books, educational materials, work plans, and other materials or directives create the curriculum of the school.

Before deciding what you will teach in your class, it is imperative that you look at your state academic standards and become comfortable with those standards for your grade level as well as the standards for your grade band. For example, if you are a 4th grade teacher, you will need to know the 4th grade curriculum, and should also be aware of what the students were previously taught (3rd grade curriculum) as well as what they will be expected to know in the next grade (5th grade curriculum). Basically, the information that the students have to learn isn't up to you, but how you teach it is where the magic and fun of teaching happens. It is important that you follow gradelevel content and provided curriculum maps to assist you in mapping out the content for the day, week, month, and semester.

Here is an example of an academic standard from the Grade 6 ELA Common Core Standards:

- W.6.2. Write informative/explanatory texts to examine a topic and convey ideas, concepts, and information through the selection, organization, and analysis of relevant content.
- Introduce a topic; organize ideas, concepts, and information, using strategies such as definition, classification, comparison/contrast, and cause/effect; include formatting (e.g., headings), graphics (e.g., charts, tables), and multimedia when useful to aiding comprehension.
- Develop the topic with relevant facts, definitions, concrete details, quotations, or other information and examples.
  - Use appropriate transitions to clarify the relationships among ideas and concepts.
- Use precise language and domain-specific vocabulary to inform about or explain the topic.
  - Establish and maintain a formal style.
- Provide a concluding statement or section that follows from the information or explanation presented.

Retrieved from: www.ade.az.gov/standards/CommonCoreStandards/default. asp.

Here is another example of an academic standard from the Grade 8 Mathematics Common Core Standards:

- F-IF.1. Understand that a function from one set (called the domain) to another set (called the range) assigns to each element of the domain exactly one element of the range. If f is a function and x is an element of its domain, then $f(x)$ denotes the output of f corresponding to the input x. The graph of f is the graph of the equation $y = f(x)$.

Retrieved from: www.ade.az.gov/standards/CommonCoreStandards/default. asp.

It is important to note that there is a difference between the term "standard" and "curriculum." The standard is the knowledge or skill that the student needs to learn. The curriculum includes the way the content will be covered and the materials that will be used to teach and assess that standard. A textbook, for instance, would be a tool used with the curriculum, but by itself would not be considered a curriculum. Math manipulatives would be a tool used within the curriculum to teach the standard. To reiterate, a textbook alone is *not* a curriculum.

The sequence of the curriculum, or order of items taught, should make sense. What is first taught should help the student understand what will be taught next. A successful curriculum sequence will be ordered so that previous knowledge helps the student learn new concepts. There should be a progression of skills and knowledge.

Most successful schools already have a curriculum in place, and expect teams of teachers to quarterly or annually discuss the curriculum and monitor the standards to ensure the curriculum is still guaranteed and viable. The terms "guaranteed and viable" basically mean that the curriculum pinpoints what content is critical for all students, sequences it in a way that makes sense and provides sufficient time to learn it, and ensures teachers attend to the content in the classroom.

These successful schools also have curriculum maps or pacing guides to help the teacher map out the content for the semester or school year. Per experts in this field (Udelhofen, 2005) curriculum mapping is "the process where each teacher records the content that is actually taught, how long it is taught, and how they are assessed and aligned to academic standards."

Depending on the school or district, some curriculum maps are created at the school level by teachers during the summer or school year, while some maps are created at the district level. Either way, it is the expectation that the teacher follows the curriculum map while still having a little flexibility based on the needs of the specific class. If a teacher is struggling to teach the content within the time provided on the curriculum map, it is crucial that the teacher talk to his/her colleagues or academic coach and get some guidance or assistance.

Table 2.1 provides an example of a curriculum map from LaRue County, Kentucky.

As you can see, the map is separated into specific parts: the timeline, the content, the concepts, the process, and the assessment. Many maps will vary depending on the school or district, but all functional maps will include the time frame (week, month, quarter, or semester), the content or skill, and the standard taught. Other items that can be included on a curriculum map include essential questions, the assessment, vocabulary words taught, and materials to be used.

Table 2.1. LaRue Country Curriculum Map

Primary 4—Traditional Grade 3

TimeLine	Content	Concepts	Processes	Assessments
	Characteristics of Organisms The learner will recognize must meet basic needs to survive. **S-P-LS-1** The learner will identify various structures and functions of plants and animals used in growth and animals used in growth, survival and in reproduction and classify these accordingly. **S-P-LS-3**	Flowering/non-flowering (flowers, cones, fruit) Amphibians Human Birds Mammals Insects Spiders	Recognize flowering plants produce seed in a fruit Recognize some plants don't have flowers Classify animals according to their characteristics Plant and animal behavior results from internal and external stimuli	TTP Relationship Report for Life Science POS 1 TTP Relationship Report for Life Science POS 3 TTP Relationship Report for Life Science POS 2
	Life Cycles of Organisms The learner will identify and illustrate life cycles of given organisms. **S-P-LS-5** The learner will recognize offspring resemble their parents. **S-P-LS-4**	Stages of flowering plant (seed, embryo, seedling, adult) Plant seeds Life cycle of non-flowering (moss, fern) (seed/spore, seedling, adult) Life cycle of insect (3 stage: egg, nymph, adult) (4 stage: egg, larva, pupa, adult) Amphibian Bird Mammal	Sequence—draw stages of growth in flowering/non-flowing plants Identify how plants make seeds Compare/contrast flowering and non-flowing plants Illustrate life cycle of a given organism Identify amphibian as a 3 stage (egg, larva, adult) Observe and identify stages of life cycle for amphibian, bird (egg, baby, adult), mammal (embryo, baby, young, adult) Define gestation and recognize different animals have different gestation periods	TTP Relationship Report for Life Science POS 5 TTP Relationship Results for Life Science POS 4

Retrieved from: www.education.ky.gov/KDE/Instructional+Resources/Curriculum+Documents+and+Resources/Teaching+Tools/Curriculum+Maps/

There is a need to persistently review and revise curriculum maps to ensure that students are taught up-to-date and valuable learning and understandings (Armstrong, Henson, and Savage, 2005). Maps lend guidance in determining what is to be taught and when it should be taught. Teachers as professionals must then decide how to best teach students a new concept or idea. Teachers at times express frustration in having so many standards to teach in the space of a year. Clustering standards and project-based learning has led to teaching smarter, not harder.

When deciding how you will teach the content, make sure you have a plan. No matter how smart or creative you are, it will only end in disaster if you don't have a plan about what you will teach, how you will teach it, what activities you will include, and how much time each activity will take. All teachers find out the hard way that if they don't use the class time wisely, the students will find a way to use it unwisely. Good planning in most cases leads to good classroom management. Depending on your team and the different expertise each member brings to the table can often lead to higher-quality lessons.

When designing a lesson, take the following items into consideration: background knowledge, the objectives, the sequence, the activities, the scaffolds, and the assessments.

Background knowledge. We will go deeper into this in future chapters, but background knowledge is crucial when learning new skills or concepts. When we learn something new, our mind makes sense of it by attaching the concept to some prior knowledge. For example, you really can't understand the concept of a waiting room without understanding the concept of a doctor's office or hospital. When creating a lesson, ask yourself "What will my students have to know in order to understand the new concept?" "How can I make a connection between this new learning and the learners' lives?" You might have to create a short, 10-minute mini-lesson to ensure your class has the crucial background knowledge needed to learn a new concept or skill.

The objective. As stated above, it is imperative that you look at your state academic standards to ensure you are teaching the concepts and skills that have been deemed necessary for your grade level. The content or performance objectives within those standards state *what students should know and be able to do.* Any important conceptual ideas or essential facts and skills should be the key information of the lesson. It is crucial that as a teacher you explain to the students what they are going to learn—it really shouldn't be a surprise (even for science teachers using exploratory methods, the students should have an idea of what they are to explore). When designing a lesson, ask yourself "What do I want my students to know and be able to do?" "What is really the point behind this lesson/standard/topic?"

As you decide on the objective of the lesson, ask yourself the following:

- Are there any high-frequency words (words that are used often) that I need to make sure to explicitly teach in order for my students to grasp the content knowledge?
- Are there any specialized terms (words that are specific to the topic) that I need to make sure to explicitly teach in order for my students to grasp the content knowledge?
- Are there any cross-curricular references (items that tie into other content areas, like mathematics, social studies, physical education, etc.) that I can incorporate into the lesson that will help the learner make connections?

The learning objective should be active. By this we mean the objective should reflect an action that the teacher can see, either through expression or action. The learning action needs to be based around the student. That is, the objective needs to start with the sentence stem "The student/students will . . ." and follow with a verb of what the student will be able to show. For example:

- Students will summarize . . .
- The student will explain . . .
- Students will create . . .
- The student will compose . . .
- Students will explain events . . .

As you can see, these learning objectives focus on the student and have the student actually acting in some manner.

The last part to a successful learning objective is deciding what the student will be using to perform the action. This is usually a noun. For example:

- Students will summarize the plot of *Othello*.
- The student will describe the purpose of the Bill of Rights.
- Students will write a persuasive paragraph on the topic of teen pregnancy.
- Students will correctly apply the Pythagorean theorem.

A well-written learning objective is active. It is based on the student, and describes an action that can be seen or assessed. There is always a possible completion—the task isn't universal and never-ending. Lastly, the objective can be built upon. That is, a new objective can be built upon the completion of the current objective.

The sequence. Just as your yearly or semester curriculum has a sequence, so should your lesson. What are the major parts of the objective/standard?

How does this connect to information they have already learned? What order will divulge the information they need to know? How will it build up so the students understand the important conceptual ideas or essential facts and skills of the lesson?

The activities. How will you teach the material? How will you involve the students in the learning? What can you do to help get the students engaged in the topic? Will you include photos, models, charts drawings, maps, graphs, timelines, or videos? How will the activities tie into the objective of the lesson?

In future chapters we will talk about how the choice of activities as well as the sequence should follow the "I do it, we do it, you do it" format. The teacher needs to model the new learning, provide time for the class to work with the new learning together, and then, if they are ready, give the class time to master the new learning by themselves. Students may not be ready for the independent learning phase until the next day, the next week, or perhaps longer. Most social constructivists recommend the "you do it together" stage where students perform the new skills within a team or small group to socially construct the new meaning before the independent learning phase. Social constructivists hypothesize that for deep learning to take place, the learners make new meaning through social interaction with others. A teacher standing up in front of a class telling students everything he/she knows on a topic does very little for the student to learn a new topic. Never again should a teacher lecture for 40 minutes and then tell the kids to complete a worksheet individually. This is not an example of good teaching!

The scaffolds. As we will discuss in other chapters, scaffolding means providing some sort of assistance as a child learns a new skill. The scaffold provides help and assistance while the student needs it, and as the student progresses, the scaffold is removed. Scaffolds can help the student process background knowledge and connect it to new concepts (concept maps), organize information (graphic organizers), or notes (chapter outlines). Many other forms of scaffolds exist and will be discussed in the book.

Tiered instruction presents students material that is a little more challenging than they are comfortable tackling alone. This creates an actual challenge for the student, but it is a challenge that they feel they can achieve. The "scaffold" is in place to support them as they continue their learning and growth (Kingore, 2006).

When designing scaffolds, ask yourself "what parts of this might the students not understand?" "How else can I teach the parts students might struggle with?" "What can I be ready to do for the students who might struggle with this?" "What can I have the proficient students work on while I work with the students who don't get it?" "What are some common misunderstandings or misconceptions that occur with this concept?"

The assessment. "How will I know if they learned it?" "What tool will I use for them to show me that they know it?" Whatever assignment you provide the students, make sure the assignment provides data as to what they understand and don't understand. Does the assignment allow the student to act out a skill or provide information at a level that is rigorous and appropriate? Most importantly, does the teacher provide checks for understanding during the lesson that will help let them know if the teaching is effective, or if the teacher needs to reflect and adjust to ensure all students are learning before progressing to the next in the instruction? Does the teacher provide prompts and feedback to move the learners forward? We will go into more detail about the importance of sound assessments later in this book.

Effective lesson planning doesn't have to be complicated, and it doesn't have to be a guessing game. Almost 20 years ago, researchers (Rosenshine and Stevens, 1986) compiled a list of effective procedures effective teachers used. This list contained the following, and can be thought of as the key pieces of effective lesson plan design:

- Quickly review the previous learning before you begin a new lesson (Recall previous information that can help students grasp the new knowledge).
- State the goals of the lesson (post the objectives of the lesson and state them in student-friendly language, provide a reason for why they need to learn this).
- Present the new material in small, logical steps and provide practice after each step.
- Provide clear and explicit instruction, demonstrations, and feedback.
- Include active practice that includes all students.
- Ask questions, check for understanding, and elicit all students to respond by signaling, talking, writing, or performing.
- Guide students during the first practice (make sure they are doing it correctly).
- Provide feedback to help with needed corrections by providing assistance and clarification.
- Monitor students during their seat work, observe the progress, and re-teach those who need it.

These nine items can be summarized as the following: The teacher shows the new learning, the teacher assists students as they try the new skills, the teacher monitors the students as they independently try the new skills, and the teacher provides useful and detailed feedback to better the independent use of the skill. That's effective teaching!

We are going to close out this chapter with an emphasis on the amount of time a teacher needs to expose a student to information before the student can really "own" the information.

Learning requires many exposures to the content or skill. If you only teach it once, the students probably won't remember it. Most research states that the average student needs at least four exposures to something to add it to his/her knowledge base (Rovee-Collier, 1995). So if the average student needs at least four exposures to information, think about the number of times a below-average student will need exposure to the content. This is why it is important for a teacher to continuously refer back to previous learning, especially within the first few days that the content was presented.

The exposure doesn't always have to come from the teacher; the exposure can also come from the other classmates. This is why it is important to use strategies like pairs or small groups within the classroom. One thing to clarify is that the exposures can be in different forms. It's okay to change up the exposure so the students can see the new knowledge in different forms. This can mean offering different exposures to similar but different mathematics problems, offering different examples of well-written topic sentences, or providing different angles of an effective free throw. So even if the new knowledge is subject matter or a skill, it is important the student is given multiple exposures to the new knowledge and time to practice it. This is called creating "opportunities to learn" (Marzano, Walters, and McNulty, 2005). The more opportunities a student has to learn something, the higher the chance for the student to gain academic success.

REFLECTION SCENARIO

It is summer, and the district has used Title I funds for teachers to meet and develop engaging and authentic mathematics lessons for the next school year. Summative data, benchmark data, and progress monitoring data show 3rd grade students are struggling with math. In addition to the dismal data results, teachers in this district are beginning to transition to the new Common Core mathematics standard. The lessons will be designed to increase student academic achievement in math as the teachers integrate the new common core standards into the content.

The 3rd grade team is meeting and planning a geometry unit. Discussion is focused on creating a lesson for the new Common Core Standards 3rd grade mathematics' strand, Measurement and Data (see the 3rd Grade Mathematics

Standard below). The grade level has come up with a project that will cluster several standards around the essential learning of understanding the concept of area and relating area to multiplication and addition. They have asked the art teacher and a couple of parents to join them in their collaboration.

The team begins their discussion by exploring several questions. What authentic learning activities will lead to deep understanding? How will they check for understanding (formatively assess) in each of the "I do it, we do it, you do it together, and you do it" phases of the unit? How will they plan for common misconceptions and what they will have ready to re-teach along the way? What other questions would you ask the team to consider that will lead to all students knowing and mastering the skills in the standard?

3rd Grade Measurement and Data Standard (AZ Academic Standards, 2010)

3.MD.5. Recognize area as an attribute of plane figures and understand concepts of area measurement.

   a. A square with side length 1 unit, called "a unit square," is said to have "one square unit" of area, and can be used to measure area.
   b. A plane figure which can be covered without gaps or overlaps by n unit squares is said to have an area of n square units.

3.MD.6. Measure areas by counting unit squares (square cm, square m, square in, square ft, and improvised units).

3.MD.7. Relate area to the operations of multiplication and addition.

   a. Find the area of a rectangle with whole-number side lengths by tiling it, and show that the area is the same as would be found by multiplying the side lengths.
   b. Multiply side lengths to find areas of rectangles with whole-number side lengths in the context of solving real world and mathematical problems, and represent whole-number products as rectangular areas in mathematical reasoning.
   c. Use tiling to show in a concrete case that the area of a rectangle with whole-number side lengths a and $b + c$ is the sum of $a \times b$ and $a \times c$. Use area models to represent the distributive property in mathematical reasoning.
   d. Recognize area as additive. Find areas of rectilinear figures by decomposing them into non-overlapping rectangles and adding the areas of the non-overlapping parts, applying this technique to solve real world problems.

3.MD.7. Relate area to the operations of multiplication and addition.

  a. Find the area of a rectangle with whole-number side lengths by tiling it, and show that the area is the same as would be found by multiplying the side lengths.
  b. Multiply side lengths to find areas of rectangles with whole-number side lengths in the context of solving real world and mathematical problems, and represent whole-number products as rectangular areas in mathematical reasoning.
  c. Use tiling to show in a concrete case that the area of a rectangle with whole-number side lengths a and $b + c$ is the sum of $a \times b$ and $a \times c$. Use area models to represent the distributive property in mathematical reasoning.
  d. Recognize area as additive. Find areas of rectilinear figures by decomposing them into non-overlapping rectangles and adding the areas of the non-overlapping parts, applying this technique to solve real world problems.

Chapter 3

High Expectations and Differentiation—The Closest Thing to a Silver Bullet

What we share in common makes us human. How we differ makes us individuals. In a classroom with little or no differentiated instruction, only student similarities seem to take center stage. In a differentiated classroom, commonalities are acknowledged and built upon, and student differences become important elements in teaching and learning as well . . . students have multiple options for taking in information, making sense of ideas, and expressing what they learn. In other words, a differentiated classroom provides different avenues to acquiring content, to processing or making sense of ideas, and to developing products.

—Carol Ann Tomlinson

Charles F. Kettering, the inventor of the electric starter, once said, "High achievement always takes place in the framework of high expectations." This also applies to teacher expectations toward student success. Teacher beliefs tend to create a self-fulfilling prophecy: teachers will get the outcomes that they expect from their students. Let's take the follow scenario as an example:

Ms. Jones is beginning her fourth year of teaching. Every year, her summative classroom achievement data reveals her female Native American students are scoring below all other classroom demographics. "They just can't do it." she thinks to herself. "They have a different culture and it doesn't blend with what we expect from our students. Just watch; it will be the same again this year."

Consciously or unconsciously, teachers often act and react differently toward students based on the assumptions they have about the individual learner's capabilities. Sociologists call this *symbolic interactionism*. A core

29

tenant of symbolic interactionism is that individuals act toward people and things based upon the meanings that they have given to those people or things.

Teachers tend to use more verifying non-verbal mannerisms like smiling, creating eye contact, and positive body language toward students who they believe are high-level achievers, and less verifying mannerisms toward students who they believe are low-level learners (Bamburg, 2004).

Studies also show that low expectations tend to go hand-in-hand with low-achieving classrooms (Cotton, 2001). In these classrooms, teachers generally view their students as limited in their ability to learn, and this view tends to create an atmosphere of failure. These low expectations can be based on past experience, empathy, or lack of ability to correct the situation. In a past experience, a teacher might have met a certain type of child who struggled and now relays that experience to other similar students.

A low expectation from empathy occurs often in teaching and tends to create a vicious cycle. We feel for students because they are so far behind. We go easy on these students and "give them a break" instead of upping the ante, increasing the intensity, and diving into a very intense and difficult teaching experience. What ends up happening is we give less work to the students that need more work, and because of this, the students fall further behind.

Teachers can also have low expectations because they don't know how to effectively have high expectations or have the tools to create an environment for high expectations.

Research also shows that when teachers increase their expectations for student success, academic gains are made (Good, 1987). There are strategies that teachers can apply to their daily activities to ensure that all students are being held to high expectations, especially for those who are thought to be at risk of failure: concentrate on offering encouragement and support to all students, monitor student achievement closely, provide useful feedback, stay away from unreliable hearsay, group students heterogeneously, communicate high expectations, give wait-time, and differentiate instruction.

Concentrate on offering encouragement and support to all students. Some students will be receptive, some won't, but as a teacher your job is to continuously encourage all students, even the ones who make it seem painful. This encouragement should not seem phony or sarcastic, but should be genuine. Provide a double-dose of encouragement for at-risk students, and share this encouragement with their family members on a regular basis. As a teacher, your interaction with students needs to be purposeful and create conditions for students to grow.

Monitor student achievement closely, and make certain that interventions are in place for students who are at risk of falling behind. By being proactive and monitoring, students can be assisted early in the unit or semester, thereby increasing their chance of mastering the learning. Future chapters on RTI and assessment will provide methods of monitoring student achievement.

Provide useful feedback. When assessing student work, make sure that your feedback explains what they did right as well as wrong, and give suggestions as to how they can improve. Based on your comments, can students explain to you how they need to improve, as well as what they are doing correctly? If students cannot repeat in their own words what they did successfully and ways they can improve, then your feedback is not sufficient.

Stay away from unreliable "hearsay" about students and their ability to learn. Stick to the data, not what other students or teachers tell you. In one of the author's first year of student teaching, a visiting teacher looked at the roster and proclaimed, "Watch out for Levi; that kid is a pain and shouldn't be in the 10th grade." Thankfully the author did not heed the advice. Although Levi was a difficult student, with extra time and effort and taking time to build a good rapport, he learned the material and succeeded in the class.

Group students heterogeneously, thereby profiting from students' weaknesses and strengths. Student grouping can be difficult and should vary depending on the task at hand. For instance, pairing your best reader with your worst reader will only cause frustration for the students and the teacher. A rule of thumb is to list the students by achievement for the specific task. Once listed, split the group in the middle and then assign partners (Smith, 2009). For instance, if you have ten students, #1 will pair with #5, #2 with #6, #3 with #7, etc. This type of grouping provides a knowledge gap between students that is manageable. Again, we cannot stress enough that grouping will depend on the activity.

Communicate to students that they have the ability to meet the standards that you hold for your class. The more often you affirm their ability to learn, the more likely they will try to meet your goals. When discussing classroom expectations, many researchers mention the "Pygmalion Effect," which means students will produce what you expect of them. For instance, if you walk into a classroom thinking "inner-city kids can't learn this concept," they probably won't. On the other hand, if your mindset is "all students in my class will learn this," they most likely will.

Allow a decent amount of wait time for student answers. This will increase the quality of answers as well as increase class participation. The rule of thumb is to provide five seconds of wait time, but more complex questions may require more time, while simple questions ("what day is it?") may only need one or two seconds of wait time. For new teachers wait time can feel awkward, and five seconds of silence can seem like a minute. Count the amount of wait time in your head, and remind students that they are not allowed to blurt answers out until you signal that the wait time is over. The chapter on active engagement will provide more detail on this subject.

Lastly and most importantly, *differentiate instruction.* Use the old analogy of getting into a house when teaching students: the easiest way into a house is through the front or back door, but you can also get into a house by using a window, crawlspace, or chimney. Be prepared to offer alternative teaching methods for children who don't learn in a conservative, traditional manner.

So what is differentiation of instruction? Basically, differentiation of instruction is shaping the instruction to meet the mixed needs of the classroom. Carol Ann Tomlinson (Tomlinson and Eidson, 2003), one of the main authorities on this topic, defines it as a way to "match instruction to student need with the goal of maximizing the potential of each learner in a given area." With all the technology and manipulates that are available to teachers nowadays, it would be a shame not to use these resources to better educate different groups of students.

Differentiated instruction has been a buzz word and research-based best practice in educational circles for over a decade, but is a concept most effective teachers have unintentionally done in their classrooms for centuries. Due to its popularity and effectiveness, many teachers are now incorporating differentiation into their instructional strategies intentionally, and a strategy becomes much more powerful when it is deliberate. These educators reflect on how diverse students encounter information and deliver the curriculum in a way best suited to the individual learner (Tomlinson, 2000). These educators take into consideration how all types of learners process information to produce meaningful and engaging projects or assignments in a safe and positive environment where learning is fostered and cherished.

Does this mean that an educator needs to teach a concept in 30 different ways for 30 different students? No. It *does* mean that the teacher needs to be able to monitor student success, and provide an alternative approach for those that need extra practice, an alternative explanation, or an advanced assignment to keep interest. It also means that the teacher needs to be *proactive* and plan flexible instructional arrangements.

Differentiation can be as simple as asking a common, open-ended question and having students apply their level of knowledge to answer it and can be as difficult as assigning different problems to different students that still meet the content objective of the lesson being taught.

Research identifies four student traits (Tomlinson, 2003) that teachers must take into consideration to promote successful learning in the classroom:

- Readiness—"A student's knowledge, understanding, and skill related to a particular sequence of learning"
- Interest—"Topics or pursuits that evoke curiosity and passions in a learner"

- Learning Profile—"How students learn best"
- Affect—"How students feel about their work, and the classroom as a whole"

Once these traits are taken into account, a teacher responds to the student's needs and differentiates through curriculum and instructional strategies:

- Scaffolding must be in place and tailored to the students as they move through the strand and concept levels of content.
- Formative assessment is the key to working smarter not harder. Formative assessments, discussed in more detail in future chapters, are continuous assessments that guide the teacher's instruction to increase student achievement.
- A tiered approach may be called for as different levels of difficulty are developed for students at varying levels of understanding. All tiers must demand a specific standards-based outcome. Said differently, no matter what the students are doing, and no matter their skill level, the lesson needs to be standards-based, be equally challenging, and have the same high-quality goal. Marian Small states it this way: "The parallel tasks have the same big idea but have different levels of difficulty, thus taking into account the variation in student readiness."
- Assignments should be focused, perceived as meaningful, and engage the student. The product must be challenging to provide the student with satisfaction of "a job well done." Although students may be working on different products, the rigor is not dumbed-down, but rather adjusted to meet the individual student learning styles.
- Teachers should present curriculum using different approaches to meet diverse learning styles giving attention to gender, multiple intelligences, and culture.
- All assignments and tasks are respectful and considered important in a caring and supportive atmosphere of learning.

In order to differentiate instruction, the teacher needs to have her finger on the pulse of the class. The teacher needs to know who gets it, who "kinda gets it" but needs more support, and who does not get it and needs much more support. In order to do this, the teacher needs to continuously get feedback from the students in the classroom. Based on the feedback, ad hoc flexible groups are created as needs present themselves across a variety of curricular areas. For example, a teacher explains to the class the concept of a verb. The teacher then asks the class to copy a sentence that is written on the board and point to the verb. The teacher walks around the classroom, and as the students write and point, she notices that ten students are not pointing at the verb. Based on this data, the teacher changes her approach. After assigning each student a partner, she directs each pair to find verbs in their story book. The teacher then brings a small group of students to her desk to work on the exercise with her additional support. Based on her assessment, the teacher has now differentiated instruction for the struggling students by utilizing flexible groupings.

Exemplary teachers deploy a variety of differentiated instruction strategies in their classrooms daily while holding all students to high expectations, and their students are the beneficiaries. This leads to a place of learning where students feel nurtured and expectations are high. Differentiation creates a community in which both the teacher and students have a sense of a learning community (Tomlinson, 2003). This leads to the type of classroom other educators want their children and relatives taught in.

There are different forms of differentiation that a teacher can use when meeting the different needs on all students (Tomlinson, 2003).

COMPACTING

Compacting consists of eliminating the reiteration of class work that has already been mastered by a student and creating new lessons that the student will find interesting and rigorous. The concept of curriculum compacting was developed in 1978, more than 30 years ago (Renzulli and Smith, 1978). The process for compacting consists of certain main steps:

1. Select the learning objectives for a given lesson.
2. Assess the class by use of a pretest to determine which parts of the lesson the student has mastered.
3. Identify students who have mastered the objectives or who might master them at a faster pace than the majority of the class based on the pretest results.
4. Streamline practice and instructional time for students who have already mastered the content.
5. Create enrichment options for eligible students.
6. Keep records of the process and instructional options available to students whose curriculum has been compacted for reporting to parents and forward these records to next year's teachers.

TIERED ASSIGNMENTS

Crafting tiered assignments consists of providing the same content to students, but varying the assignments based on their ability or challenge levels. Again, even though the assignments are tiered, they should be equally challenging. For example, you don't want one student to write a report about the impact of the Civil War, while another student draws a picture of a horse. In her book, *Differentiating Instruction in the Regular Classroom: How to Reach and Teach All Learners,* Diane Heacox provides six ways to structure tiered assignments:

- *Challenge Level*—Use Bloom's Taxonomy (knowledge, comprehension, application, analysis, evaluation, and synthesis) to guide the task at different levels of challenge.
- *Complexity*—Although students may be working on the same assignment, the teacher varies the complexity (simple to complex) of the assignment based on the student's level of mastery.
- *Resources*—The teacher varies the resources used by reading levels and complexity of content.
- *Outcome*—Although students may use the same resources, the outcome may be more advanced for advanced learners.
- *Process*—Although the outcome may be the same for all students, the teacher shows a simpler process for students needing more assistance and requires advanced learners to reach the same outcome through a more difficult process.
- *Product*—The teacher can assign various products to be graded, ranging from verbal and linguistic, visual and spatial, logical and mathematical, bodily kinesthetic, or musical (Heacox, 2007).

INDEPENDENT STUDY

Independent study provides a student an opportunity to independently work on a project that interests them yet meets the goals of the overall lesson. It is crucial that before any independent study takes place that the teacher and student have an agreed upon list of outcomes and clear expectations for the project. In many schools, an independent study contract is created and signed by the teacher and student. This contract lists the assignment expectations. Items like note taking, outlining, interview skills, letter writing skills, research skills to locate, record and organize information are included in the task.

LEARNING CENTERS

Learning centers provide areas around the classroom where students can work on different tasks simultaneously based on a similar topic. Learning centers can also be used to as enrichment tools for students who finish assignments early. These centers must be very organized and preplanned by the teacher to be effective, and norms and discipline procedures should be discussed as a whole class to keep disruptions at a minimum. Centers should change from theme to theme in order to complement the specific topics covered in the classroom. The centers should be focused, perceived as meaningful, and engage the student.

FLEXIBLE GROUPINGS

Flexible groupings have been around since the days of the one-room school house, yet many of today's teachers do not incorporate them into their teaching. In flexible groupings, students are grouped on an hourly, daily, or weekly basis based on specific needs or mastery of content.

Flexible grouping usually starts with whole-group instruction, and then, based on the mastery of content, the teacher creates temporary groups based on their need to review, practice, re-teach, or enrich. This allows gifted students to work on engaged real learning, while those who need review or more practice are not left behind. The groups can be created by readiness, interest, reading or skill level, background knowledge, or social adequacy. Remember: flexible grouping should only be temporary! The groups should be based on student need, and should change depending on the task at hand.

REFLECTION SCENARIO

During a parent-student-teacher conference early in the school year, the parent of a gifted student brought up how her son, Sam, was disengaged from learning and reported feeling bored with assignments in Ms Parker's 7th grade Social Studies class. The family traveled widely and made it a point to research future destinations with their children before they visit new countries or regions. This prompted Ms. Parker to reflect on her practice of a one size fits all approach to teaching middle school social studies that is aligned to state standards. What could she do to re-engage Sam and provide for other students who might already come in knowing the content of a particular unit of study from the standards-based curriculum?

Chapter 4

Assessing School and Classroom Climate

Safety is something that happens between your ears, not something you hold in your hands.

—Jeff Cooper

It is the responsibility of every adult . . . to make sure that children hear what we have learned from the lessons of life, and to hear over and over that we love them and they are not alone.

—Marian Wright Edelman

At this point, we have discussed the areas crucial to teaching: classroom management, high expectations, and the importance of differentiating information. Another item to take into consideration is improving the climate of your school and classroom. School improvement is an ongoing goal that affects every school in the nation, no matter what label or status applies.

Every school and classroom should continuously try to do better than the year before, making sure that the current class learned more than the last one. One way to ensure that learning and improvement efforts will continue is by creating a healthy school climate in your building and creating a healthy classroom climate with students.

Getting the kids in class is the first step to giving them an education and setting the climate of the class. If the kids aren't present in your class, it is impossible for you to educate them. Every class period is an opportunity for your students to learn, so a day absent from school is a day absent of learning. It's common sense, but students who attend class on a regular basis tend to learn more and have greater success in school—imagine that!

So why do students not attend school? Many factors can come into play. It could be they don't understand what's being taught, and would rather not be present than look stupid. This is important because more than 8 million students in grades 4–12 read below grade level (National Center for Education Statistics, 2005). Equally shocking, only 15 percent of low-income 8th graders read at a proficient level.

It could be that they have other things that are more pressing in the immediate future, like working to put food on the table for their family or having to babysit other siblings. One role of the teacher is to let the students know they are missed when they are absent and see what the school can do to increase attendance. The key is to not punish the student for not being in school—this is counterproductive. The success will come from finding out the root cause for the absences and fixing it. This can come from parent conferences, extra tutoring, community outreach and assistance, or be as simple as making a connection with the student. We will go into student attendance in more detail in the next chapter.

Research shows a direct link between a school's success and the presence of an optimistic, nurturing climate (MacNiel, and Maclin, 2005). In today's world, distractions such as gangs, poverty, abuse, and other ailments can affect the student body, and therefore change the culture of the school. It is crucial that schools and teachers try to minimize the impact these items have on the learning institution. One of the most effective methods to do this is to create ways for all students to be involved in the school.

When students find a meaningful role in their school, they are less likely to engage in disruptive behavior than students who feel out of place and deprived of individualized involvement. Within the individual classrooms, teachers can assist by building a rapport with students and being a positive, non-judgmental role model. The National Longitudinal Study of Adolescent Health, a study of 90,000 middle and high school students, found that students who have strong and quality relationships with teachers are more likely to have heightened academic achievement as well as better behavior and attitude (Harris, Mullan, Udry, Muller, Chandra, Reyes, Pedro, 2010). These students also were less likely to use drugs, commit suicide, join gangs, or show other at-risk behaviors. Similar studies have found similar results (Verdugo and Schnieder, 1999).

For example, when Oran Tkatchov, one of the book's authors, taught high school, a student named Angel was a well-known gang member and disturbance in the school. Although Oran and his co-teachers were not able to change Angel's lifestyle, they were able to build a relationship with him. After a year and many, many conversations, based on the relationship which was built, Angel was able to tone down his gang presence in the school.

Because the teachers built a respectful relationship with this student, he understood that the teachers had a job to do, and his actions were making their job difficult. Because the teachers got to know him and he got to know his teachers, all parties saw each other as human beings and were able to get past the gang member versus "The Man" struggle.

Teachers can help keep students interested in school by providing a challenging and engaging curriculum. Students are most motivated to learn and display the sense of success and achievement when they are able to succeed at tasks that they find interesting and widen their capacities. For example, Dan Southard, a high school teacher in Arizona, used Clive Barker horror novels to engage a group of 11th grade "goth" students who were threatening to drop out. After assessing that they had the ability to complete the assignments but decided not to out of boredom, he made a connection between Clive Barker and Edgar Allan Poe that led to the students reading classic literature and writing a literature review comparing and contrasting the two mediums.

Engaged students also tend to have better school attendance and lower drop-out rates (Finn, 1989). After providing an engaging curriculum, there are other steps teachers can take to improve the culture in their school and classroom.

The first step is to reply to students in a caring and supporting manner. As stated in the first chapter, in the beginning of the year create rules regarding behavior and homework, and consistently implement and provide reminders of these rules—again, again, and again. Many students who struggle in school do not have structure in their lives. By providing it at school, some students will find the structure to fill a need.

Remember that you are a role model. Let me repeat that—you are a role model. Model the behavior you expect from your students and consider this as important as the teaching of academic standards. Similarly, as a teacher you might be the only "responsible citizen" the student interacts with. It is important to show how a responsible adult acts. This can include how a responsible person acts when frustrated, how a responsible person acts when mad, how a responsible person acts when disappointed, or even how a responsible person acts when faced with conflict. Lastly, as a role model, the teacher needs to show and discuss the successes that can be achieved by getting an education.

Remember to reward good behavior and sanction unacceptable behavior. Positive messages need to outweigh the negative. For at-risk students, try to provide a 4:1 positive message to negative message ratio.

Another step a teacher can take to improve the school's culture is to participate in the development of a school safety plan, discipline code, and mission statement for your school. This will not only let you influence the policies of your school, but you will also get to know what your colleagues deem as important and some history of prior school safety plans, discipline programs, and mission statements. Ask your principal if there are any committees you can join.

Take time to explain instructions to students. Make sure they understand what it is you are expecting them to complete. Follow "I do it, we do it, you do it" to ensure they are capable of completing a task without your assistance.

Coordinating with other teachers can also increase a positive school culture just by increasing teacher collaboration. Talk to other teachers in your building about what they are assigning so students aren't overwhelmed. Ask other teachers about individual students to see what has been working and what has been ineffective.

Although giving specific feedback on assignments is important for all students, it is extremely important for students who don't like school. Explain to students why they did a great job on an assignment, or specifically explain how they can improve. Based on your feedback, the student should be able tell you what they did correctly, what needs to be corrected, and how to correct it.

Many different school districts and states have tools to help schools and teachers assess the school culture, climate, and communication. For example, the Arizona Department of Education has created the *Standards and Rubrics for School Improvement* (Arizona Department of Education, 2005), as a tool to be used by schools across the state in order to identify the strengths and limitations of their overall program. The indicators are defined within the following four standards: Leadership; Curriculum, Instruction, and Professional Development; Assessment; and School Culture, Climate, and Communication. The Standards and Rubrics for School Improvement are anchored in the scientifically research-based principles and indicators that consistently distinguish top-performing schools.

CLASSROOM AND STUDENT SURVEYS

Per Arizona's *Standards and Rubrics for School Improvement*, in order to create a robust school culture and climate, the school must function as an effective learning community, supporting a climate conducive to student achievement, and possessing an effective two-way communication system. The authors believe the best way to assess the climate of a school is to ask the students, parents, and teachers how they feel about the school. This can be done through surveys, and then the data can be disseminated to show where the strengths are as well as the weaknesses of the school's climate. The survey questions would obviously vary based on the audience (student, parent, teacher, etc.), but some issues addressed in the survey could include:

- School support of academic achievement
- Community awareness and input
- Safety
- School organization
- Class schedule
- Professional development
- Shared decision making

- Interaction between students and adults
- Fairness
- Discipline
- Resources
- Respect and Trust
- Morale
- Growth

At the school level, parents should be updated by monthly or bi-weekly newsletters explaining what is occurring at the school. This newsletter can be a means to get parent feedback. As an educator, feel free to survey your students throughout the year, after units of instruction, or quarterly. Surveys could include questions about the clarity of the information, class arrangement, the level of engagement, and so forth.

IMPROVING CULTURE BY PARENT INVOLVEMENT

Research over the last decade tells us the same thing: parent involvement can assist student achievement (Epstein, 1987). No matter the ethnicity or socio-economic background, when a parent is involved in his child's education, the student tends to earn higher test scores, attend school more frequently, exhibit sound behavior, and remain in school until graduation.

Many important programs and policies to include parents and community in a school's culture are set by the school or district and not the teacher. These can include addressing the community's needs (food, shelter, etc.) or providing facilities for cultural activities (church sermons, fiestas, etc.). Many family and community news letters are also published by the school and district. These news letters can keep the community up-to-date on school functions, and also provide a listing of ways the community can assist the school.

Although the school and district usually take the lead on parent engagement, there are also many things a teacher can do to supplement or support the school or district's effort to involve families. Based on the comfort level of the parent, involvement can include something as minimal as the parent verbally expressing to their child that they have academic expectations or asking about what they learned in school, or can include something as substantial as providing after-school tutoring, or volunteering to assist as a teacher aide.

Teachers can include parents by trying to meet with them at least once face-to-face per year, provide materials or suggestions on how parents can assist their children at home, and telephone the parents when the student is having problems or has accomplished major success. Although we should be trying to increase all forms of a parent's involvement in a child's life, the key role for the teacher is to find a way to link the parent to the student's academic learning.

Parents who had a bad experience in school or even dropped out might feel intimidated by a scholastic setting, or feel like they have nothing to offer. These parents can assist teachers by merely:

- Asking their child about the school day and what was taught in the class.
- Making sure a quiet place and time are available for homework.
- Scheduling a healthy time for the child to go to bed and wake up during the school week.
- Talking to the child about the importance of education, and in upper grades talk about post-high school opportunities including college.

Teachers can also include parents by not accidentally excluding them. The "ah-ha" story this book's authors heard about came from a veteran teacher who worked in a school located in a lower socioeconomic area. The school was making a concerted effort to use academic vocabulary and make the students speak in proper, complete sentences. When a student spoke improperly, teachers would correct them by saying things like "no, speak like you're educated" or "educated people don't talk like that." What they didn't realize is that these students would then go home and tell their family that they weren't educated or they were stupid. This ended up unintentionally making the parents and the community feel unwelcome and even spiteful toward the school. Once the teachers and administration became aware of this, they changed their response to "Because this is a school, we will speak academic English within the building. At home or with your friends you can decide the best way to communicate." For us, this story drove home the importance of how messages to children and parents are to be crafted but also how fragile the school-community partnership can be with some populations.

So how can you tell what the best types of parent involvement you should try with your students' parents? As a teacher, start by finding the definition of what "parental involvement" means at your school or district, and then try to give examples of opportunities within the school for parents to get involved. You might find out that there are no opportunities for parent involvement, hence the lack of parental involvement.

Another important thing to remember is that some cultural, educational, and language issues can become barriers to parental involvement. A report by the California Department of Education stated that schools must actively acknowledge and respect parents' culture, as well as inform these parents of the way the American education system works and what opportunities are available for parent involvement (Ramirez and Douglas, 1989). Also remember, parents lacking a high school education might feel embarrassed to enter your school, or feel that they have nothing to offer as far as support.

The Parent Institute (Wherry, 1996) offers these suggestions for getting parents involved in the classroom:

- Help parents understand they are the most important teacher in their child's life. It is said that from birth until high school graduation, a child will spend 15 percent of their time at school, and 85 percent of their time at home. Politely explain to parents that they are the most influential educator of their child, and their views on education will affect their child's view on education.
- Provide a list of ways parents can help in your classroom or with their child's education. In some cultures, parents would never think about interfering with the school. Let parents know they are welcome to assist, and provide various opportunities in which they might be able to lend a hand.
- Keep it brief when you send information home. Keep it to one page in length, and use a 6th grade reading level. The longer your requests, the less chance parents will read it. Send things frequently, but keep them short.
- Have a plan. Don't say you want parents to help, and then have no way they can help you. Figure out different ways you could use parents depending on the amount of time, education, and skills they have.
- *Thank them!* Always go out of your way to send a card or e-mail even after you thanked them personally. Parents are busy, so make sure they really understand how thankful you were for them coming in and helping out!

Below we have listed various suggestions to increase parent involvement. Some of these can be accomplished at the teacher level; others will need to be accomplished at the administrative level. In case you need more information, we have added where the information originally came from.

Fourteen Ways to Improve Parental Involvement:

1. Flood them with information,
2. Make it a school-wide effort,
3. Recognize students and parents,
4. Involve students in recruiting parents,
5. Conduct participatory projects that include the entire family,

6. Recruit community members,
7. Make the classrooms and the school a comfortable place,
8. Use the telephone as an instrument of good news,
9. Find out why parents are not involved,
10. Have a variety of event scheduling plans,
11. Operate a parent hotline,
12. Use community members to endorse the program,
13. Videotape programs for parents, and
14. Provide support services like babysitting. (Dan, 1995)

Strategies for Getting Middle School Parents Involved:

- Develop a policy for parental involvement,
- Make sure that at least one person in the building knows every child well,
- Maintain a friendly school office,
- Encourage parent-to-parent communication,
- Hire a full-time parent contact person,
- Have a parent room in the school building,
- Determine and meet family needs for services, and
- Provide translation services when appropriate. (Berla, Henderson, and Kerewsky, 1989).

Sixteen Parent Involvement Strategies:

1. Involve parents in mutual goal setting, contracting and evaluating;
2. Involve parents in assessment of school policies, practices and rituals;
3. Open a parent lounge, center or resource room;
4. Develop public information displays, public service messages and work site seminars;
5. Develop a parent handbook of guidelines and tips;
6. Hold a weekend or evening public information fair;
7. Have a parent and student exchange day;
8. Award extra academic credit for parent involvement;
9. Have an old-fashioned family night at school;
10. Develop a school-wide communications plan;
11. Keep parent-teacher dialog journals for communication;
12. Engage in official parent proclamation efforts;
13. Assemble monthly home achievement packets;
14. Conduct home visits for a special bond;
15. Enact a school-wide homework policy; and
16. Have a meet and greet program for involvement. (Schurr, 1992)

REFLECTION SCENARIO

A new principal has come to Windcatcher Elementary School. The school is in a low-SES Latino neighborhood. The principal asks each grade level to host a meeting for their classroom parents to teach parents how to understand their child's data, from progress monitoring data to proficiency test results. How would you plan the meeting? What is your agenda for the night? What support would you need from your district and principal? What are some strategies to ensure a good parent turnout? What would be your follow-up during the year?

Chapter 5

Student Mobility and Attendance

Those who get lost on the way to school will never find their way through life.

—German Proverb

The only real security that a man can have in this world is a reserve of knowledge, experience, and ability.

—Henry Ford

If students are not present in your class, it is very difficult for them to learn what you are teaching! The more students are absent, the more they fall behind and the more difficult it is for the teacher to help students catch up. Poor attendance creates gaps in the child's learning, a lack of continuity in the learning, and increases the chance that the child will eventually drop out of school. Most reasons that students miss class fall into four categories (Baker, Sigman, and Nugent, 2001):

1) Family. Sometimes families don't value education, or aren't aware of the importance of being in school on a daily basis. Sometimes the family structure is dysfunctional (drugs, lack of supervision), which hinders a child's ability to get to school.
2) School. Items within the school can cause students to not want to attend. Things like bullying, teacher attitudes, class size, or school culture can make the school an unfavorable environment.
3) Economics. The cost of transportation or the necessity to have a job can limit a student's ability to regularly attend school.

4) Student's ability to learn. Things like emotional and physical health issues will create attendance issues. Also, if a student is struggling to keep
   up with the class, the chance of not attending regularly increases.

Most attendance issues or policies will be created at a school or district
level. As a teacher, it is important to familiarize yourself with these policies. Ideally, your school or district will have a way to identify, contact, and
counsel chronically absent students. Most schools will try to contact these
students first by phone, and then at times by an actual home visit. To promote
attendance, some schools and districts will provide incentives, such as fairs or
parties for the students with good attendance. Incentive like these tend to help
students who are attending to keep attending, but do little for the students who
are already missing a lot of school, especially at the high school level.

As a teacher, what can you do to keep attendance up in your class? The
no-brainer to this is you need to monitor your attendance. The assumption of
the authors is your school will expect you to do this on a daily basis by taking
class attendance. If your school doesn't require you to take daily attendance,
the authors suggest you still do it as a best practice. By taking attendance, the
teacher is relaying to the students (A) they are expected to attend, and (B) that
the attendance of the students is important to the teacher.

As mentioned in other chapters, make sure what you teach is engaging
and that the students are connected to the learning. The more students are
engaged, the more they'll want to attend the class. Once students are disengaged, the chance they will miss school increases, especially in the high
school level. Think about it: how often do you overlook something you enjoy
doing? By human nature, we are attracted to things we enjoy or challenge us
and avoid things that are boring, stressful, or seem unachievable.

We are also attracted to those people who seem sincerely interested in what
is best for us and avoid those that seem to not care. By connecting students
to the learning and showing our students the passion we have for the subject,
we can create a much more inviting classroom climate. One of the most
important things a teacher can do to ensure students will arrive to class is to
make the class inviting. Make sure students feel valued and know you appre-
ciate them attending your class. This is just as important if you are teaching
kindergarten or teaching a college course.

So how should a teacher react to a student who is consistently absent from
school? If a student tends to be absent, do not punish him, since there can be
so many reasons that can influence attendance. Punishment is rarely ever an
effective strategy. The option of after-school or before-school tutoring can
be used to counter the time the student has missed. Ask the student privately
why he has missed so many classes. Based on his answer, you or the school

counselor might assist the student with the barriers preventing him from attending school on a regular basis.

One thing for certain is at the teacher and school level there needs to be early interventions with students who are attendance-challenged. Someone needs to get involved, promote a positive relationship with the student, and find a way to increase attendance. As stated earlier, this could be done with an incentive program. Remember with incentives, try to stay away from materialistic items. Try things like, "if you make it to class all week, you'll have the option of either redoing a quiz for a higher grade, using the hall pass for an additional five minutes, or deciding what game we play during recess." The most important thing is to try to build a relationship with these kids so they know you care, and that they don't think they are "just another face in the school." Students who feel like they have a role in the school tend to attend more often.

Another way to intervene is by contacting the student's family. This strategy works well at both the elementary and secondary level. When contacting a family member, a phone call is usually the first step. In this conversation, state the amount of times the student has been absent, explain the students presence has been missed, and give details about what the class has learned while the student was out. Make sure to state that the student's lack of attendance is noticed and her participation is missed. Ask the parent if there is anything the school (not you, the individual) can do to assist them in getting their child to school. Based on the parent's answer, decide if their recommendation is practical and contact your administrator if needed. The recommendation could be as simple as "Sarah feels intimidated by Thomas and hasn't been wanting to attend since the new seating chart was implemented," or as difficult as "our family car has been repossessed; we have no way of getting her to school unless her aunt picks her up." In the first scenario, the teacher can possibly make a change to address the situation. In the second scenario, a school counselor or administrator should be contacted to assist in finding a solution.

If the phone call does not help increase student attendance, talk to the school counselor or principal about a home-based intervention. Please do not do a home-based intervention without consulting your counselor or principal first! Due to safety reasons and the possibly delicate situation, your school principal or other office personnel should be brought into the conversation. These home-based interventions can address issues like transportation, housing arrangements, sleep schedules, homework times, the importance of education, truancy laws, and so on. Again, these interventions shouldn't seem like a scolding or a punishment but used as a positive way to increase the parent's awareness of the situation and the student's ability to get to school.

Student mobility, or the unscheduled moving of a student from school to school for reasons other than promotion, is a prevalent problem across the entire country and is the cause of many students not attending school regularly. During an average K–12 education, most children make at least one non-promotional change in schools (Rumberger and Larson, 1998). National data in 1994 showed by the third grade, over one-half million school kids had attended more than three schools (Office of Juvenile Justice and Delinquency Prevention). Unfortunately, these frequent changes link to lack of achievement, poor test scores, and even referrals to special education (Alexander, Entwisle, Dauber, 1996).

Mobility tends to affect some subgroups more than others. The majority of students who suffer from mobility are from the inner city or high-poverty homes, with some urban schools claiming student turn-over rates as high as 80 percent (Stover 2000). ELL students also tend to have a high mobility rate. On average, poorer students tend to struggle academically, so a high rate of mobility adds to the chance of a downward academic spiral. A study of 10,000 high school students found that mobility between the 1st and 8th grade for *all* types of students increases the odds of becoming a dropout (Stover 2000).

Most mobile students go through inter-district transfers, meaning that they leave a school from one district and go to another school in another district. In a recent study, inter-district transfers for mobile students were twice as much as the intra-district transfer rates. In smaller schools, a small number of mobile students can impact performance (National Report to Parliament on Indigenous Education and Training, Department of Education, Science and Training, 2001). No matter the size of the school or district, it's hard to keep records accurate or accessible if the population is very mobile. This makes it hard to assess where a student is academically, and what supports need to be in place to assist them.

Some states have a higher mobility rate than others, as well as different types of mobility. For example, Colorado has more urban mobility, Missouri has more urban mobility, but Nebraska, Wyoming, and Arizona see more rural mobility. For instance, the mobility in a distant, rural locale might occur for different reasons than the mobility of an intercity school. Most mobility "hot spots" have poverty above the state's mean. This high mobility occurs when parents have to move when trying to find work, or have to move when losing their current housing situation.

Over the last five years, poverty and the economy have created an increase in student mobility. States like Arizona and California have seen people leave as the housing market crumbled, while places like Wyoming saw an increase in student enrollment as energy jobs were created during the same time span.

Smaller mining towns tend to continuously have a mobile population as old mines close and new mines open (Fong, Bae, and Huang, 2010).

So what can a teacher do to help decrease mobility rates? Research shows that the best factor in decreasing mobility is increasing the overall quality of the school and classroom (Rumberger and Larson, 1998). If parents believe that the school is helping their child learn and providing a nurturing environment, they are less likely to transfer their child to another facility (McCarthy, and Still, 1993). For instance, after completing a comprehensive school reform, Hollibrook Accelerated School in Houston, Texas reduced its mobility rate from 104 percent to 47 percent.

Here are some suggestions for teachers and administrators to help limit student mobility:

- Speed up the process of integrating a student into a new school as much as possible.
- Create "buddy systems" by partnering new students with current, productive students. This will increase the student's role in the school and help the student feel like they fit in.
- Make a follow-up appointment with parents two weeks after the student transfers into the school to discuss how their child is adjusting to the new school.
- Provide outreach to educate parents about minimizing the negative effects of mobility. The more parents are educated about how student mobility can decrease student achievement, the more parents will try to find ways to keep their child in the current school or school district.
- If the change in schools is inevitable, urge the parents to keep their children in the same school for at least the remainder of the school year, and offer guidance to resolve any problems that are provoking the student transfer.

REFLECTION SCENARIO

James has been absent three days this week and has a history of extended absences. His sixth grade teacher phoned James' house and found that his mother had asked him to stay home to watch his brother, a third grader, who is home with the flu. The mother is a single parent and must work to support the family. How would you handle the situation? Are there students in your school who have had absentee issues? What is your district's policy regarding absenteeism?

Chapter 6

Time on Task and the Importance of Student Engagement

The most successful man in life is the man who has the best information.

—Benjamin Disraeli

All men by nature desire knowledge.

—Aristotle

The average student in the United States spends around 179 days in school, but how much of this time is actually spent on learning? A 1983 study found that only 60 percent of the school day is spent on instruction, and that girls spend more time engaged in learning than boys (Rossmiller, 1983). Another study presented scarier statistics, showing that only one-half of the school day focuses on actual instruction (Honzay, 1986). In a time where international benchmarks and comparisons are headline news, these numbers are not acceptable. As a teacher, in the beginning of the year you might look at the curriculum and say "I can't get this done in the time provided." By increasing time on task, your students will learn more and discipline should improve. By increasing the opportunities for students to learn, the teacher is increasing the opportunities for the student to succeed.

Time on task, or the percentage of time students are engaged in learning, is crucial to student test scores, especially in higher brain-functioning classes such as mathematics or foreign languages (Brewster, and Fager, 2000). The more time students are engaged in a subject, the better chance they will comprehend that subject in a deeper, more rigorous, and more thorough manner. This makes perfect sense. No matter if the topic is cooking, playing the guitar, or golf, the more time you spend engaged in the subject the more you will know about it.

So what are some things that can cause time *off* task? Here are a few items guaranteed to make you lose instructional time (Smith, 2009):

1. Lack of a plan. If you are making stuff up on the spot, you will lose time. Without a plan, the students will be confused, you'll be explaining things over and over, and time will be lost. Remember: great teachers model what they expect from their students. If we expect our students to be prepared to learn, we need to be prepared to teach by having a plan.
2. Bird walking. Bird walking is a nice way of saying getting off-topic. has All teachers have a soft spot that they love to talk about. My Spanish teacher could ramble on about cooking. A weakness of one of this book's authors was football. By wandering off-topic, we lose instructional minutes. As teachers we need to make sure the majority of time with our students is focused on the academic standards, not other topics.
3. No structure. As stated in Chapter 1, structure is crucial to effective teaching. Without structure in a class, the teacher will spend too much time trying to organize the chaos than actually teach the students the necessary content.

In order to increase time-on-task with the classroom, educators should begin to focus on three factors: physical needs, teacher preparation, and curriculum.

PHYSICAL STATE OF THE STUDENT

Students' physical states influence their ability to learn, so it is important that teachers and school districts ensure that every student is properly nourished. Studies have shown that students who eat a healthy breakfast perform with better speed and accuracy in responding to problem-solving tasks (Pollitt, 1991).

Another study by Harvard University and Massachusetts General Hospital confirmed these findings, as well as concluded that children who regularly ate breakfast had better behavior, and were less hyperactive than children who skipped breakfast (Murphy, Wehler, Pagano, Little, Kleinman, and Jellinek, 1998). By doing something as simple as providing granola bars or fruit to students, teachers and principals can increase the chances that their students will spend more time learning in the classroom. If a teacher feels a child does not have a stable home environment which provides food, shelter, and sleep, the teacher should contact the school counselor to find what is available for assistance. Most schools have federal or state Free and Reduced Lunch programs to assist students that cannot afford regular nutritious meals.

TEACHER PREPARATION

As stated above, good teacher preparation can save plenty of time. Teachers should go out of their way to model classroom rules, praise students who are on task, and not waste quality teaching time by grading papers, planning lessons, or getting into verbal confrontations with students who aren't paying attention. The most important thing a teacher can do to increase learning time is clearly state classroom rules, and enforce those rules on a consistent basis (Walker, Audette, and Algozine, 1998). As stated in Chapter 1, rules should be stated in a positive manner and should also be short and easy to understand. Remember: classroom teachers can also let students help define the rules, as well as the consequences for breaking the rules. Teachers need to explain to the students why the rules are in place. If students understand the rationale behind the rules, there is less chance the student will break them.

Lastly, remember that the way teachers organize their classrooms can increase student engagement. Studies have shown that by arranging seats to address the task at hand—for example, U-shaped for classroom discussions, rows for test taking—students will remain engaged for a longer period of time (Bonus and Riordan,1998).

ENGAGING CURRICULUM

Finally, curriculum plays an important role in increasing time-on-task. Students will be more engaged in learning if it relates to their lives, and includes real-world situations (Lumsden, 1994). By doing this, school work will seem pertinent and worthy of their efforts. By creating the connection between what is being learned and how this assists the student in life, the teacher is creating a link into the student's interest.

Curriculum should also be challenging, yet realistic (Brewster and Fager, 2000). Many student distractions occur when a child is bored or overwhelmed by the material. Teachers should evaluate the difficulty of what they are teaching, and monitor the class to see if the material is engaging to their students.

Student engagement is as close to a silver bullet in education as there will ever be. There are often moments in a school day when we as educators are struck by the many blank expressions staring at us from the ranks of students we are committed to teaching. At these times, we reach into our magical bag of tricks and pull out the most alluring ditty we have to change this catatonic state of monotony to the alert state of student engagement. Many experienced teachers can improvise, but it does take up precious instructional time to react, reflect, choose, and execute a strategy that will eventually save the day. Does it not make more sense to intentionally plan for student engagement from the very beginning? Active engagement has been defined (Bonwell and Eison, 1991) as "instructional activities involving students in doing things and thinking about what they are doing."

In a recent survey, 40 percent of high school students stated they were bored in class due to material they didn't find relevant to their lives, and 60 percent of prospective drop-outs affirmed lack of value in schoolwork as the main reason for possibly leaving high school (Yazzie-Mintz, 2006).

It comes as no surprise that high engagement in learning has consistently been linked to reduced dropout rates and increased levels of student achievement (Blank, 1997). Below are some suggestions to keep student motivated in class, some which have already been reviewed within the book and are being emphasized again due to importance (the authors hope that the reader can see that many of the best practices that have been addressed benefit many different areas within education, which is why they are called best practices).

Suggestion #1: Students who feel their teachers are supportive and cared about their success are more engaged in class and have higher success in their learning (Heller, Calderon, and Medrich, 2003).
Building students' confidence is not blindly telling them they are doing a great job every day, but assessing weaknesses and strengths and delivering critiques in a timely manner that can increase their skills to complete the task at hand. A good teacher increases the self-efficacy in their students. Self-efficacy means a person has confidence that they will be successful. By providing specific feedback to students, the teacher increases their self-efficacy by superficially mapping how the student can get better. This is done by making the successes and errors transparent and providing ways that the errors can be corrected.

Suggestion #2: Stay away from extrinsic rewards, like candy bars, pencils, soda, etc.
Intrinsic motivation is motivation that occurs from the inside; we are intrinsically motivated when we have the feeling of self-accomplishment or discovery. According to Robert Marzano "when students are working on goals they themselves have set, they are more motivated . . . and they achieve more than they do when working to meet goals set by the teacher."

If a student feels a task is important and the chance of success is high, there in an increased amount of intrinsic motivation applied to the task (Marzano, Pickering, Arredondo, Blackburn, Brandt, and Moffett, 1992). For the task to be deemed important, it has to satisfy a personal goal or assist us in achieving a personal goal.

This ties in to why teachers should state the learning objective that is being taught. If the student knows what they are to be learning, and if the teacher emphasizes how this learning can be used in real life, the chances of the student being intrinsically motivated to learn the subject will be increased.

Extrinsic motivation comes from the outside, such as a reward or something materialistic. In order for something to be considered a reward, it must be expected and have commercial value (Tileston, 2004). Try to limit gifts and rewards. Gifts should be related to the task accomplished. Also, reward efforts that truly deserve to be rewarded. Giving a prize for minimal success relays to the student that minimum effort is adequate (Brooks, Freiburger, and Grotheer, 1998). Thanking a student for doing what they are supposed to do should be acknowledged (a simple "thanks for doing this," or "I see you have your pencil out and are ready to learn, excellent") but probably isn't worthy of a reward.

Suggestion #3: Ensure that classroom expectations for performance and behavior are clearly posted and consistently applied (Skinner, and Belmont, 1991).
As previously stated, it is crucial that a teacher explains what is expected, models what is expected, and continuously applies what is expected.

Suggestion #4: Help students understand the criteria for individual assignments by providing a rubric; explain to them how each piece was graded (Strong, Silver, and Robinson, 1995).
Promote mastery learning whenever possible (Anderman, and Midgley, 1998). Rubrics, which will be described more in a later chapter, provide students with the criteria for a certain grade or point range. Rubrics make the assignment expectations clear.

Suggestion #5: Work to build quality relationships with students (McCombs, and Pope, 1994).
With at-risk students, try to talk with them for two minutes a day for two weeks about any appropriate topic they find interesting. This will help build a relationship with the child and provide the teacher with a deeper knowledge

of the child's interests and background. Taking the time to build a relationship with students shows them that you care about them as individuals. These one-on-one relationships cannot be stressed enough. They are the building blocks to effective classroom climate and culture.

Suggestion #6: Evaluate students based on the assignment, not in comparison to the rest of the class (Anderman and Midgley, 1998).
This is also another reason to use a rubric. Students should know they are being evaluated based on set criteria, and not the teacher's personal preference. Students should clearly understand and see evidence that they are not being judged against their peers, but are being evaluated based on their performance of grade-level criteria.

Suggestion #7: Provide students with the chance to respond to questions and work in groups.
The more students respond and discuss their learning, the more they increase their understanding of the skills (Mastropieri and Scruggs, 2000). Use techniques for active engagement (see below) such as choral response, peer tutoring, hand signaling and partner-reading to keep students engaged in the assignment.

ENGAGEMENT TECHNIQUES AND ACTIVE PARTICIPATION

The amount of engagement the average child receives during the day can be staggering: cell phones, text messaging, Tweets, DVDs, GameBoys, streaming video, MTV, TIVOs, color TVs, 3-D TVs, iPods, video games, Wiis, X-Box, Playstation, or the web. For us as educators to think that a child can sit still for 90 minutes listening to a teacher talk about a strange subject would be foolish.

According to CNet, in 2008, the average 13–17 year old sent and received about 1,742 texts a month (Reardon, 2010). Today's kids expect information fast, and can digest it in different forms. By no means are we saying that teachers need to entertain the students, but teachers do need to make a conscious effort in involving the students in the learning.

If a teacher does not engage students in the learning, problems will occur. This is a guarantee. Most classroom disruptions don't occur because the "Bart Simpson" in the room was born a troublemaker. Classroom disruptions occur because students who don't understand would rather be seen as being troublemakers than being stupid, bored students are causing trouble as a form of entertainment, and then there is a small portion of students who just want someone to pay attention—and they'll get that attention any way possible. Engaging students in the learning can alleviate all three of these issues.

When students are asked to do something, to interact, or to participate, they have less time to daydream, entertain themselves, or wander off cognitively. Also, when students are actually engaged in doing something academic, the teacher can see if the students are doing it correctly and help the students learn what they are supposed to know. If a teacher is just lecturing and the students are just listening, it is difficult for the teacher to assess if the students actually understand the content, or if they are really even listening (we all know how easy it is to act like we are listening when, in reality, we aren't paying the slightest bit of attention). When teachers ask students to do something and get involved, then the child is getting the attention and is more engaged in the actual learning.

At this point, a teacher might say, "I ask them to do things, but they don't." This is true in many classrooms, but if you follow the three suggestions below, the majority of students will be with you and do what you ask:

(A) What you ask them to do can't be just busy work. Giving them a list of vocabulary words and asking them to find the definitions in the dictionary won't hold their attention; it wouldn't hold *your* attention if you were asked to do it.

(B) Make sure they are *able* to do what you are asking them to do.

(C) Support them as they are doing it. Don't just assign something and think you can sit down and grade papers.

After the teacher gets the students engaged in the learning, the teacher will need to always monitor and correct, monitor and correct, monitor and . . . well, you get the point. Usually, the teachers that get the best results in their class are always on their feet, moving around, sitting with students, showing examples, while positioning themselves in the classroom where they can see what the rest of the class is doing.

As a teacher, no matter what the grade, you will have the class clown one-liners, the students who act like you are pulling their teeth every time you ask them to do something, the kid who always has to say "this is stupid"; that's just part of the clientele we serve. These minor offenses can be handled in a way that doesn't disturb the class structure. Also, as teachers, we need to decide which battles to fight, and when to fight them.

If there is a specific behavior in the classroom that we don't like from the class or a specific student, we need to find a way to change that behavior. Screaming "stop it!" tends not to work. Researchers recommend teachers follow the following five steps (Mather and Goldstein, 2001).

1. Define the behavior. Why is it happening? When is it happening? How often does it happen?
2. Design a way to change the behavior. For example, "The student tends to act up after lunch. Maybe if I make sure to include a hands-on activity immediately as they come in, the behavior will stop."
3. Track if the change is working.
4. Most importantly, praise the new behavior. Once a student is behaving properly, let them know. "I see you are at your desk quietly writing in your journal. Thanks."
5. Consistently apply whatever you did that changed the behavior.

By consistently having students engaged in their learning, you as a teacher have broadly applied step five across your entire classroom, therefore pre-correcting many student behaviors and being proactive in your classroom management. As the year goes on, there will be other items you'll have to adapt, but keeping student engagement in mind as you create lessons will save you a lot of trouble right out of the gate.

Before teachers can use techniques for active engagement, they must focus on broader issues. First, make sure you are prepared (Jackson and Davis, 2000). It sounds simple, but just as in sports, the team with the best game plan tends to win. When preparing, think about:

- The curriculum. Do you understand the content, know how you are going to teach it, and how you will assess the learning?
- The teaching objective. What is it you will be teaching? Is any background information needed to learn it?
- The plan. In what order will things be taught? What materials are needed? What do the students already know? What should they know when you are done teaching it?
- Expectations. Are you asking them to learn something new? Are you being rigorous while still being realistic as far as what can be accomplished within the timeframe? Are the learning targets and activities appropriate for your classroom students?

Think of engagement in two ways. One, getting them involved or to comply, and two, getting them into what you are teaching. Sometime both are possible. This would be the ideal situation. Sometimes just getting them to comply is a winning situation, and some would argue that compliance must come before they can really become engaged. In this section, we will discuss ways to get students involved in the learning. The authors of this book believe that active engagement, or compliance, is very important and crucial for any learning to take place.

Research over the last 20 years has relayed that more learning takes place in classrooms where students are engaged. Student engagement is defined as the students' willingness to participate in scheduled school activities, such as attending classes, submitting required work, and following teachers' directions in class (Chapman, 2003). In classrooms where student participation is required and not an option, increases in work completion, attendance rates, as well as lower behavioral problems take place (Voke, 2002).

Successful student engagement does not "just happen"; it must be preplanned by the teacher. First, the classroom must present a positive atmosphere for learning. When engaging students, teachers must allow enough "wait" time when expecting an answer, dignifying wrong responses, repeating a question, or giving hints that will encourage students to try again (Marzano, Pickering, Arredondo, Blackburn, Brandt, and Moffett, 1992).

Student engagement has four specific attributes (Fitterer, Harwood, Locklear, Wright, Fleming, and Levinsohn, 2004). The teacher must:

- Elicit *all* students to be engaged in the learning *at the same time*
- Elicit students to be engaged in the academic learning
- Ensure student engagement is *mandatory* for all students throughout the learning
- Maintain engagement of all students

There are six basic ways to engage or actively involve all students in academic learning: speak, write, signal, perform, think, and combination (Smith, 2009, Fitterer, Harwood, Locklear, Wright, Fleming, and Levinsohn, 2004).

Speaking is the ability to talk during the classroom session. When creating lesson plans, teachers must actively create time for students to talk about the content discussed.

Writing is the physical motion of putting thoughts on a page. By stopping to have students write or fill in a graphic organizer, the teacher is engaging the students into the learning process with a physical (although minor) activity.

Signaling is a physical motion to a question or topic. This can be as easy as the child putting a "thumbs up" if they think a statement is correct.

Performing is providing some sort of physical motion to the content. This can include students mimicking the way a cell divides, or types of mnemonics.

Thinking is a covert form of engagement which can be provided by the teacher giving students think time to process a certain term.

Combination refers to two or more of the above being used at the same time.

Once students are engaged, they can remain engaged by active participation techniques.

TECHNIQUES TO INCREASE ACTIVE PARTICIPATION

Choral Responses. Choral responses occur when the class as a whole repeats an answer or term out loud. Choral responses are best used when the reply will be short and exact, and should not be used when responses are long-winded or can vary (Smith, 2009).

If students are looking at the teacher, the teacher should ask the question, put her hand up to indicate silent think time, and then lower her hand while saying "everyone" as cues to respond. When doing this, the teacher should use the same hand motion and cue word daily, therefore creating a habitual method of instruction in the classroom.

If students are looking at a common stimulus, the teacher should point to the stimulus, ask the question, give think time, and then signal for the response (Archer and Hughes, 2011).

If students are looking at their own book or paper, the teacher should have the students point to the section in the book being taught, ask the question, and then use the auditory signal to elicit the response. If students don't respond, repeat the instruction. Make sure the student have been given adequate wait time, and give a signal (thumbs up, look at the teacher) when they have had enough wait time.

Partners. Much research shows that student achievement increases when students are allowed to occasionally work in pairs. When assigning partners, the teacher needs to create the partnerships and not allow students to choose who they will be partnered with. The teacher should pair lower performing students with middle performing students. (For instance, the student ranked #1 will be paired with #15, #16 with #30, etc.) Each partner should be given a number and needs to physically sit next to the person they are partnered with (Smith, 2009).

Partners can be used in various ways. The partners can say answers to each other, retell the content of a story, review content, brainstorm, explain processes, strategies, of examples, or even read to each other. Before partnering, make sure students have been taught how to work together, and teach students how to give and receive encouragement and compliments. Remind the students that these are learning partnerships, and are not based on friendship. Change the partnerships occasionally (every three to six weeks) and let the students know the groups will be changed on a regular basis.

Think/Pair/Write/Share. In Think/Pair/Write/Share, the teacher asks a higher-order question and then provides time for the students to individually think of a reply. Students then pair with a predetermined partner and discuss their thoughts regarding the question while the teacher wanders the room to assess the student conversations. The students then agree to an answer to the question, write it down, and share it with the group.

Think/Pair/Write/Share provides all students the opportunity to discuss the concept as well as learn from each other (Smith, 2009). In order to effectively pull off a Think/Pair/Write/Share, remember to follow these steps:

Think

- Have students think and record responses.
- As students are writing, walk the room and record their ideas and names on an overhead transparency.

Pair/Write

- Have students share their ideas with their partners. Have them record (write) their partner's best ideas.
- As students are sharing, continue to record ideas on the overhead.

Share

- Use the transparency for sharing with the class.

The authors provide an example of a Think/Pair/Write/Share later in this chapter.

Because the student response has a higher chance of being correct after working with a partner, students will tend to not shy away from stating their response in front of the class.

Written Responses. When having students write, make sure that the length of the written response is sufficient to avoid dead time. In other words, make the response fairly short or make the response endless to keep students from wandering off after completion. When completed, have students put their pencils down to show completion or turn their paper over.

Other ways to quickly and effectively actively engage students include the student touching or putting pencil on stimulus, which allows the teacher to monitor the attention to the stimuli; acting out or recreating an event just taught; using hand signals to share categorical responses; and displaying answers with response cards.

ACTIVE ENGAGEMENT WHEN PASSAGE READING

Choral reading is similar to choral response in that the entire class is reading the same thing at the same time. The teacher notifies the students where in the text to begin, and then reads the selection aloud with the students. The teacher needs to read at a moderate rate, and remind the students that their voice volume should be the same as the teacher.

In *cloze reading*, the teacher reads the passage, but occasionally stops on a word and the class is expected to say that word out loud (Rye, 1982). The teacher should stop on meaningful words, and avoid items such as pronouns or conjunctions.

Silent reading occurs when the each student reads the passage to themselves silently. Before it begins, the teacher should pose a pre-reading question, and then wander the room as the students silently read (Garan and DeVoogd, 2008). The teacher tells students to read a certain amount and asks them to reread material if they finish early. Silent reading should be monitored. This can occur by having individuals whisper-read to the teacher if the teacher taps their shoulder, as well as by posing a post-reading question for the class to answer.

Partner Reading occurs when the teacher assigns each student a partner (see above for partnering), and the reader whisper-reads to partner. Students alternate by sentence, paragraph, page, or time.

Students will learn more, retain more, and remain engaged when they actively participate in the learning (Akey, 2006). When *student engagement* is alive and well, *teacher engagement* is also increased and everyone ends each school day with a sense of accomplishment and a feeling of satisfaction.

TIPS FOR BETTER LECTURES

All educators and administrators must lecture sometime in their careers. Unfortunately, some rely on lecturing as the primary way of delivering information to their students, but research has surfaced disputing the effectiveness of this method of imparting knowledge to the masses.

A research study assessed student learning directly after a lecture to see how much students retained. The results showed that students remembered 70 percent from the first 10 minutes. The disappointing news was that the students remembered just 20 percent from the final 10 minutes of the lecture (McKeachie, Pintrich, Yi-Guang, and Smith, 1986). Many times educators wait until the end to deliver the most crucial information.

In 2006, the High School Survey of Student Engagement (HSSSE) was given to over 81,499 students from 26 states. In the survey, two-thirds of the high school students said they were bored in class every day. When asked why, 75 percent stated "the material wasn't interesting to me" and 31 percent said they had "no interaction with the teacher." (Yazzie-Mintz, 2007). Another study found that students retain more if the teacher talks for six minutes or less (Ruhl, Hughes, and Schloss, 1987). Other research (Penner, 1984) found that the average attention span for a *college student* is between 10 and 20 minutes, so image what it would be for an average high school student!

Although we might like hearing ourselves talk, most people, let alone school kids, will begin to cognitively drift away and lose engagement. In order to keep this from happening, there are a variety of active engagement instructional strategies to employ when delivering content, and many are preferred over lecturing (Smith, 2009). Although there are many alternatives to lecturing, there are times and situations when lecturing is the best way to convey information. The following list provides suggestions to enhance lecturing:

1. Begin the lecture with an interesting question or pose a problem that can be solved using the information that will be provided.
2. Ask questions throughout the lecture and respond in a positive manner to the answers.
3. Provide written focus questions, lecture notes, a lecture summary, or graphic organizers to the students prior to lecturing.
4. Have students share answers with a partner for questions posed during the lecture.
5. Add joy to the lecture by including humor. Just because something is academic doesn't mean it has to be stone-cold serious.
6. Stay on course and tie in previous student knowledge.
7. Use appropriate tools such as live demonstrations, videos, PowerPoint presentations, and other multimedia.
8. Incorporate "Think/Pair/Share" and let students discuss portions of the lecture as groups to break up the lecture.
9. Keep a brisk pace throughout the lecture.
10. Do not read the lecture to the students. Reading continuously from notes does not allow dialogue and processing time for students to make important connections (Smith, 2009).

Combining the above strategies and tips while lecturing will ultimately lead to livelier lessons and more meaningful learning that students will retain over the long term. Another way to engage students is to have them take responsibility for their learning. This works especially well with older students. Give choice in the assignments. For instance, provide a general topic, like weaponry in World War II, and then provide a due date as well as a few non-negotiable about the assignment. Have the students check in weekly for a progress report. If a student misses a deadline, have them provide an explanation of why they missed it and how they will make it up. By empowering the students to make decisions, their engagement in the assignment will increase. Suddenly, the assignment is personal.

Motivation has three key parts: autonomy, mastery, and purpose (Pink, 2011). When we allow students to have a choice in assignments, we are focusing on all three of these items. Autonomy basically means they have a choice; they have to make a decision. Mastery means they will be getting better at something. Purpose is they are driven to complete the assignment because they are actually interested in the topic.

DIRECT INSTRUCTION VS. INDIRECT INSTRUCTION

Direct instruction means the instruction is teacher-directed or teacher driven. When "classroom teaching" comes to mind, direct instruction is what most people think of. Direct instruction can consist of lectures, but can also be any instruction where the teacher is discussing or modeling a topic or procedure. When using direct instruction, the students should have something to do besides just listen or watch the teacher. Graphic organizers are a perfect compliment because they show the student how information connects, how the information is arranged, or what information is the most important to learn.

SAMPLE ACTIVITY—THE JIGSAW

The jigsaw activity has been around for decades, and is a useful way to use cooperative learning in all grades, including adult learners. To begin, break the class into smaller groups, and the students in each group are numbered. For example, the assignment is to read a chapter discussing the five parts of a plot. The class is broken into four groups with five students in each group. Each student in the group is given a number:

At this point, the teacher assigns each number a task:

"Ones will read and take notes about conflict, twos will read and take notes about rising action,threes with read and take notes about the climax, fours will read and take notes about the falling action, and fives will read and take notes about the resolution."

As the students read, the teacher walks around the room monitoring the class and assisting when needed. Once the students read and take notes on their assigned portion of the assignment, the students with the same assignment from the other groups get together to compare the information:

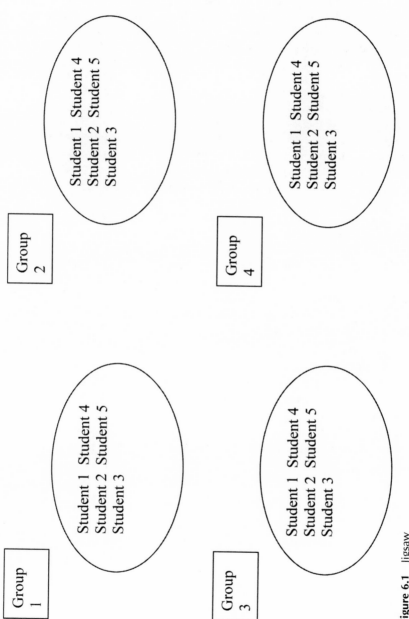

Figure 6.1 Jigsaw

"All ones meet in the west corner of the room and compare notes. Make sure you all agree as to what is the most important information. All twos meet in the east corner of the room and compare notes. Make sure you all agree as to what is the most important information. All threes meet in the north corner of the room and compare notes. Make sure you all agree as to what is the most important information. All fours meet in the south corner of the room and compare notes. Make sure you all agree as to what is the most important information. All fives meet in the center of the room and compare notes. Make sure you all agree as to what is the most important information."

As the students meet and discuss, the teacher monitors the room, and assesses each group's understanding by listening to their conversation and correcting if needed. After the groups have had time to meet and discuss, the teacher directs them to get back into the original four groups:

"Wrap up your thoughts. At the count of ten please be back in your groups. One, two, three . . ."

Once the students reconvene in the groups, they are responsible to share their information with the others, and take notes from what the rest of the team has to share. For example, student one from group 1 is now responsible for sharing his information about conflict with the rest of group 1. Then student two from group 1 is responsible to share her knowledge of rising action with the rest of group 1.

The jigsaw technique is an easy way to get students involved when a decent amount of reading is required. As the groups share, the teacher walks around the room and monitors the conversations. Once the activity is over the teacher can review the essential knowledge. The only major drawback of the jigsaw is it takes time. Also the teacher should always assign the students to groups, and make sure the students are arranged with peers that will best advance the learning.

SAMPLE ACTIVITY: THINK/PAIR/WRITE/SHARE

Think/Pair/Write/Share is a great four-step strategy that ensures all kids can be called upon and provide an answer if called upon. Teaching starts by asking a question:

"What are the attributes of a circle? Think about the question and write down your thoughts."

By providing the students think time, the teacher is giving the students time to devise a quality answer and make connections between the question and what they know. As stated earlier, the amount of think time will vary based on the complexity of the question. Next, the teacher directs the students to pair up. As stated in earlier chapters, students should know who their partner is in the beginning of the year, semester, or class.

> "Turn to your partner and share your answer. Discuss your ideas. Put a check next to any ideas you both wrote down. If your partner has any new information and you both agree it's correct, write it down."

As the students pair and share their answers with their partners, the teacher walks around the room to monitor the activity and correct and misconceptions. The teacher can also write down some of the answers provided and share with the group. By having the students share answers, the students can safely see if they are "on the same page" and can be reassured they have an answer to share. Once the students have been given adequate time to share, the teacher brings the class back to attention.

> "You have five seconds to end your sentence and bring your attention to me. One, two, three . . ."

Once the attention is back on the teacher, the teacher can call on a group to share their answer, or state some of the items the teacher heard.

> "Excellent job. Suzy and Alfred said a circle is round. That's correct. If you didn't write that down, please do so know. Jamal and Adam said a circle doesn't have a pointy edge, like a triangle does. This is correct as well . . ."

Think/Pair/Write/Share is a great alternative to calling on random students or posing a questions and asking students to raise their hands if they know the answer. Think/pair/share can also be modified to write/pair/share, read/pair/share, watch/pair/share, or even listen/pair/share. This can be used often within a class, and gets many students involved instead of only the "high-flyers" or the "blurters." To reiterate for importance, it is necessary that the students know who their partners are in order for this strategy to work seamlessly.

REFLECTION SCENARIO

The art teacher reads over his notes on artist Marc Chagall. He has already posted the objective on the whiteboard the night before—Objective: Review and Discuss Marc Chagall. The students are in for a treat. This is one of his favorite artists and he has so much information that he could talk for hours on the subject. He glances at the clock—10 minutes to go before the students arrive. He turns on the projector, dims the lights, and readies his notes on the lectern.

The bell rings and students arrive. The classes are small at this charter. He only has 9 students this semester at the high school.

The students slide into their seats in the darkened room that has the colorful Marc Chagall print shining on the whiteboard. Mr. Smith takes attendance quickly as students quietly talk with one another. And then Mr. Smith is up in front of the class welcoming his students and enthusiastically introducing the artist, Marc Chagall. He talks about the context when Mr. Chagall lived and asks how that affects the content of his art. One student begins to answer, but Mr. Smith goes on. Mr. Smith is progressing through each slide and describing each colorful print as it focuses into view. Students at the back table are quietly doodling. Another student at the back is texting with her phone under the desk. A student at the front rests her head on the desk, peeking up at the painting. Mr. Smith is gesturing and pointing out the fabulous symbolism in the artist's work. He thinks to himself that he really has the rapt attention of his students today. The students are so engaged in the art of Marc Chagall.

Are the students engaged, and how do you know? What is the evidence? In what ways might you change Mr. Smith's lesson to ensure engagement and be able to check for understanding?

Chapter 7

Understanding the Multiple Intelligences

To learn without thinking is labour in vain. To think without learning is desolation.

—Confucius

Knowledge speaks, but wisdom listens.

—Jimi Hendrix

Howard Gardner (Gardner and Hatch, 1989) defines intelligence as "the capacity to solve problems or to fashion products that are valued in one or more cultural settings." Although his work may not be as widely used as it was in the 1990s and 2000s, it is still important in the realm of education in that it reminds us that all children do not learn the same and that all children have intellectual strengths that differ from one other. Gardner's research postulates that there are eight different types of intelligence. The eight multiple intelligences are:

1. Verbal-Linguistic Intelligence. This intelligence is characterized by strong verbal skills, as well as verbal sounds and patterns. A student who can easily recite information or explain a situation would be strong in this area. Poets, authors, and lyricists would fall into this category.
2. Mathematical-Logical Intelligence. This intelligence is characterized by spatial thinking, conceptual thinking, and the ability to distinguish numerical or logical patterns. Students with this intelligence can perform intense calculations and see connections between different items. Accountants and even computer programmers would fall into this category.

3. Musical Intelligence. This intelligence discerns pitch, timber, rhythm, beat, or the ability to reproduce or manipulate sound. These students can create melodies, or easily improvise over another piece of music. Musicians and composers have this intelligence.

4. Visual-Spatial Intelligence. This intelligence is characterized by the creation of images or pictures; basically anything visual. These students can create graphic representations of information and mentally form information. Artists, structural engineers, and designers would have a strong visual-spatial intelligence.

5. Bodily-Kinesthetic Intelligence. This is characterized by physical movement, or the ability to control the body or imitate something physically. These students can mimic movements and are not clumsy. Athletes and dancers would fall into this category.

6. Interpersonal Intelligence. Interpersonal means the ability to read other people, work well within groups, or respond appropriately to others. These students can work within a group and "have their finger on the pulse" of those around them or those they are watching. Psychologists, counselors, teachers, and hostage negotiators are strong in this intelligence.

7. Intrapersonal Intelligence. This intelligence is characterized by an ability to be self-aware, and have an understanding of one's own needs and feelings. These students tend to "take things up a notch" and use much higher-order thinking when answering a question. Poet, psychologists, or philosophers would be examples of people with high intrapersonal intelligence.

8. Naturalist Intelligence. This person has a strong ability to care for living things, or understand the sensitivity of the outdoors. These students seem to be one with nature and understand the cycle of life. Biologists, forestry professionals, and river guides would have a strong naturalist intelligence.

In many cases these intelligences will overlap, and for most regular students they will. For example, most good writers will show strong verbal-linguistic strengths as well as intrapersonal skills. Most mathematically savvy students will excel in both logical as well as spatial activities. As a teacher, you can provide questionnaires to students regarding their intelligence strengths (there are tons of these to be found on the Internet) or in time, as you get to know your class, you will see the different intelligence strengths of your students naturally appear.

Don't feel the need to incorporate all eight intelligences into one lesson. Be aware that there are many intelligences, and keep track of which intelligences your activities tend to include. If one intelligence is not being implemented regularly, take note and address that intelligence in an upcoming lesson or activity. Try to incorporate activities throughout your classroom that provide an arena for more than one intelligence to shine at a time (Williams, Blythe, White, Sternberg, and Gardner, 1996). Make sure to hold all students accountable for the activity, even if the activity is not built around an intelligence that is their strength, or provide an option of activities that still assess the same learning goal. To say that an athletic student does not need to complete the naturalist Physical Science assignment because it does not contain any bodily-kinesthetic outlet would be downright silly.

USING THE MULTIPLE INTELLIGENCES TO ADAPT YOUR CLASSROOM INSTRUCTION FOR VISUAL, AUDITORY, AND KINESTHETIC LEARNERS

As we know and research supports, the ways that students process information varies from student to student. Most studies conclude that the majority of students learn information in three modalities: visual, auditory, and kinesthetic. Researchers (Reiff, 1992; Stronck, 1980; Eislzer, 1983; Meier, 2000) have concluded that in a regular classroom, the students would be approximately:

- 25–30 percent visual learners
- 25–30 percent auditory learners
- 15 percent tactile and kinesthetic learners
- 25–30 percent mixed modalities (most mixed modalities are a mixture of visual learners combined with one of the other two.)

Therefore, only 30 percent of the students will remember most of what is said in a classroom lecture and another 30 percent will remember primarily what is seen.

In this chapter, we will discuss the three types of learning modalities, and include ways to enhance classroom instruction for each group.

Visual learners rely on pictures to remember things and can recall better what they have observed or read. Chances are this will be the largest group of learners in your class. They love graphs, diagrams, and illustrations. They want to know what the subject looks like. Teachers can best communicate to them by providing handouts, diagrams, mind maps, bulleted lists, word webs, videos, visuals, and other forms of graphic organizers. Have students use highlighters to mark important words or information. Try not to give only oral instructions without accompanying notes or visuals.

Colors and pictures can be very effective tools to reinforce learning for visual learners. Videos and other forms of media arts are successful vehicles of learning for these types. Tools to use when teaching could include movies, television, streaming video, pictures, posters, murals, maps, charts, field trips, computers, demonstrations, and experiments. Visual learners tend to struggle with names and have problems remembering rules or directions that are not written down.

Visual Products:

- Dioramas
- Drawings
- Flow Charts
- Storyboards
- Advertisements
- Movies
- Plays
- Maps
- Designs
- Collages
- Sculptures
- Paintings

- Slide shows
- PowerPoint presentations
- Bulletin Boards
- WebPages
- Pamphlets
- Cartoon strips
- Photo journal
- Data Tables
- Graphs
- Banners
- Mobiles
- Storyboard

Auditory learners listen carefully to all sounds associated with the learning. Very few people are solely auditory learners. They enjoy listening, but cannot wait to have a chance to talk. Auditory learners learn best by listening and talking aloud. They are good at remembering things that they hear. They often read to themselves as they study. They are also often distracted by noise and sounds. Auditory learners tend to be good storytellers. These kids remember names and places. These students react well to lectures and discussion; in fact, they almost need to discuss what they read in order to remember it. Teachers can best communicate with them by speaking clearly and asking questions. Verbal repetition is a helpful means of studying for auditory learners.

Teachers should provide oral instructions for assignments, even if the instructions were previously provided in writing. Include whole group and partner discussions in your class when applicable (Deci, Vallerand, Pelletier and Ryan, 1991). Provide students with videos or audiotapes to complement written text. Allow time for students to read out loud or talk out loud when problem solving. Provide breaks from silent reading periods. Tools to use when teaching: read-alouds, debates, discussions, interviews, lectures, books on tape, plays, radio, podcasts, and music and songs.

Oral Presentations:

- Plays
- Debates
- Dialogues
- Newscasts
- Podcasts
- Commercials
- Threads

- Speeches
- Acting
- Interviews
- Story Reading
- Skits
- Oral Reports
- Songs

Kinesthetic learners, sometimes called somatic learners, learn best through touching, feeling, and experiencing what they are learning. Kinesthetic learners need movement and action. Kinesthetic learners benefit from sitting at the front of the class to help them to stay focused. Some kinesthetic learners seem fidgety, having a hard time sitting still in class. Many kids who are diagnosed with Attention Deficit Disorder or Attention Deficit Hyperactivity Disorder are kinesthetic learners. They like realistic applications and process information best from hands-on, team activities and animation, including changing seats and moving around (Jones, 2007). They remember best by writing or physically manipulating the information (Meier, 2000). These learners generally do not like lecture or discussion classes, but prefer to actually "do something."

Bodily-Kinesthetic Products:

- Build a machine
- Create an experiment
- Dance
- Field trip
- Game

- Role Play
- A show
- Exercise Routine
- Demonstration

Teachers should vary instruction not only from day to day but also within a single class period and provide students with many opportunities to complete hands-on work. Allow students to role play to gain further understanding of key concepts. Provide students with the opportunity to work in small discussion groups as they study materials (Stronck, 1980). Kinesthetic learning can be enhanced by including active learning strategies like taking notes while listening to a passive lecture. Tools to use when teaching: games, models, dioramas, manipulatives, letters, Scrabble, arts, experiments, and field trips.

REFLECTION SCENARIO

Ms. B teaches a poetry unit each year that is aligned with the English Language Arts Standard. She has always had students write and recite their poems in presentations before their classmates. This year she asked students what they thought of a coffee shop where students can perform poetry in a variety of ways. Students elected to act out poems, wove poetry into original songs played with guitars, and presented videos they created reading their poetry in the background. Reflect on units that you have taught in the past. In what ways might you give students opportunities that involve multiple intelligences? Reflect on a lesson you will teach next week. Where might you be able to add more variety in reaching your students throughout the lesson by integrating at least three multiple intelligences?

Chapter 8

Accessing Background Knowledge

Exploring the old and deducing the new makes a teacher.

—Confucius

Before you can really start setting financial goals, you need to determine where you stand financially.

—David Bach

Students are constantly faced with new information, especially in the upper grades. To effectively process this new information, students must construct an understanding of vocabulary, create paradigm shifts, and deconstruct prior misunderstandings.

The ability to perform these tasks relies on *background knowledge* to make sense of new information, as well as help students categorize and make connections of what is being learned. Many great educators have long ascribed to the philosophy that curriculum materials and background knowledge are part of the foundation for academic success.

Students lacking sufficient background knowledge or those who cannot activate prior knowledge may struggle to contribute and achieve throughout the curriculum, where reading to learn is crucial for success (Strangman and Hall, 2004). A strong correlation is found between prior knowledge and reading comprehension (Langer, 1984).

We acquire background knowledge through:

(1) Our ability to process and store information and

(2) the number and frequency of our academically oriented experiences, or the number of experiences that will directly align to our knowledge of content we encounter in school (Marzano, 2004).

Dr. Anita Archer, one of the foremost experts in reading instruction today includes "Vocabulary and Background Knowledge" as one of the "Building Blocks of Reading Instruction" (Archer and Hughes, 2011).

Recommendations to increase student background knowledge include:

- Engage students in meaningful activities that incorporate prior learning. Spend time before lessons making connections.
- Include activities that reflect the cultural diversity of your classroom and provide the application of multiple intelligences.
- Use graphic organizers as a tool to help students trigger prior knowledge and categorize new information.
- Use cooperative grouping to share prior knowledge between students.
- Involve community members as educational peers, and create mentoring relationships. This will create tutors with residential and cultural similarities to struggling students (Marzano, 2004).
- Use the streaming videos available to provide students with images of other countries and past events. When taken in small collaborative groups guided by the teacher, "virtual field trips" can build background knowledge, engage students in academic dialog, advance higher order thinking skills, and increase vocabulary development (Mandel, 1999).
- Constantly evaluate classroom instruction to ensure you are building on what students know, and correcting any misconceptions they might have.
- Utilize pre-reading activities, such as discussing the content of a story, linking a common experience, and explaining problematic lexical items relevant to their reading materials. (Droop and Verhoeven, 2003)

Regarding vocabulary and background knowledge, effective instruction should accomplish the following:

- Begin with student-friendly information about the word's meaning.
- Immediately prompt students to use the word.
- Keep bringing the words back in a variety of formal and informal ways.
- Get students to take the word learning beyond the classroom.
- Help students use context productively. (Beck, McKeown, and Kucan, 2003)

Researchers William Christen and Thomas Murphy proclaim, "It appears that providing students with strategies to activate their prior knowledge base or to build a base if one does not exist is supported by the current research. It is our contention that this is one way teachers can have a positive influence on comprehension in their classrooms" (Christen and Murphy, 1991).

One important part of accessing background knowledge is providing a student time to access the knowledge. As stated in previous chapters, the term "wait time" means the time given for students to recall information. In the field of education there are basically three types of wait time (Lipton, Wellman, and Humbard, 2001) a teacher should be aware of:

1. The amount of time the teacher pauses after asking a question. Based on the complexity of the question, this time can range from two seconds for an easy question to five or six seconds for a complex question. This time allows the student the opportunity to actually think.
2. The amount of time the teacher pauses after providing a response. This time allows the student to make sense of the response and organize it with their background knowledge of the topic or similar topic.
3. The amount of time a teacher pauses before responding to a comment or question. This pause shows that the teacher is thinking and models good practice. It is a gesture to show the question deserves a well-thought out answer.

This seems simple, but sometimes it is difficult for a teacher to wait five seconds after asking a question. Also, waiting before jumping in with an answer can be difficult. Make sure to consciously wait after asking questions or answering complex questions so the student has time to process it.

Although student engagement will assist in creating increased student participant in school, connections still need to be made between old knowledge and new knowledge for students to truly immerse themselves in the learning. Students are continually faced with new information in school, and students need time to process this information and make sense of it before they can learn even more new information (Chall, 1983).

Remember that in order to effectively learn, students must construct new understanding of material, create paradigm shifts, and deconstruct prior misunderstandings. The ability to perform these tasks is essential to learning because background knowledge is used to make sense of new information and to help us categorize and make connections of what is being learned. In the field of education, there is a strong correlation between prior knowledge and reading comprehension (Echevarria, Vogt, and Short, 2000).

REFLECTION SCENARIO

A 5th grade teacher in a rural classroom in Hawaii introduced the book about Balto, the sled dog, who was instrumental in getting a diphtheria antitoxin from Anchorage to Nenana, Alaska to prevent an outbreak of the disease. The Iditarod is the sled dog race that is run each year to commemorate the feat. Many children had never even been out of their village. How might the teacher scaffold the students' lack of background knowledge to make the reading of the story of Balto more meaningful? Share strategies for helping add to your students' background knowledge and what have been most successful for you.

Chapter 9

Vocabulary

All Teachers Need to Teach It
and Teach It Well

When I approach a child, he inspires in me two sentiments; tenderness for what he is, and respect for what he may become.

—Louis Pasteur

The aim of education must be the training of independently acting and thinking individuals who can see in the service to the community their highest life achievement."

—Albert Einstein

I do it, we do it, you do it.

—Anita Archer

Many teachers search for strategies that will aid their students in developing a rich vocabulary and raise the students' comprehension and academic achievement. Researchers postulate that "explicit instruction" in vocabulary will achieve positive results for our diverse populations of students (Archer, 2007). Research shows that orally tested vocabulary was a significant predictor of reading comprehension ten years later (Cunningham, and Stanovich, 1997). By the third grade, students with limited vocabulary have waning comprehension scores in the later elementary years (Chall, Jacobs, and Baldwin, 1990).

On an average, a preschool child from a professional family is provided annually experiences with 11 million words, a working class family 6 million words, and welfare family 3 million words (Hart and Risley, 1995). Vocabulary assessed in the first grade predicted over 30 percent of reading comprehension variance in 11th grade.

Research implies that direct vocabulary instruction is not a staple in daily teaching activities (Dunn, Bonner, and Huske, 2007). Only seeing a word will not help the learner master it. Students need to hear the proper pronunciation, practice saying it aloud, and also create their own definition (Ellis and Beaton, 1993). By saying and using the word, the student will have a better grasp of the term and also store it in memory (Fay and Cutler, 1977).

A teacher's first instinct to assist students who are struggling with vocabulary might be to simplify the assignment, or limit the amount of words the student needs to read. In many cases, this is what we remember our teachers doing for struggling students when we were in school. In reality, this is one of the worst things a teacher can do. By limiting the vocabulary of a struggling student, the student will get further behind, while advanced students will get further ahead. This has been called "the Mathew effect," basically meaning that "the richer get richer as the poor get poorer" (Archer, 2007). What a good teacher needs to do is provide the same vocabulary to all students, but provide effective instruction as well as scaffolding for the students who need a little more assistance.

For a single vocabulary word, assuming the need of mastery is worth the time, teachers should first provide a description and example of the new term. Next, ask students to restate the description or example in *their own words*. This is important as they attach their own background knowledge to the new term. If necessary or if the term is abstract, ask students to construct a picture or graphic representing the word. Finally, create opportunities for the students to use the word, and as the teacher, make sure to use the word when you speak.

Evidence tells us that after the early elementary grades, a sharp decline in interest in reading occurs (McKenna, Kear, and Ellsworth, 1995). One reason is classroom texts after the third grade tend to be more rigorous in information, and students need to use effective strategies to figure out the meaning or to gain understanding. Unfortunately, many of our struggling readers have not mastered these strategies for successful reading. By teaching students methods to decode text and assignments, teachers can limit the number of students who will become disinterested and unmotivated to read. Effective vocabulary instruction is more than just giving the word's definition. As a matter of fact, this would be considered ineffective vocabulary instruction.

It is important that students use the words in various ways and describe the words in various ways, including the creation of what the word means as well as what the word doesn't mean. Students should also represent the new words in linguistic and nonlinguistic forms. A script for a teacher to teach a word could look like the following:

Teacher asks—"*Can you figure out this word?*"

Don't waste tons of instruction time having the students struggle with the word. If they can't get it, move to the next step:

Teacher tell—*"This word is _____. What word? Reread the sentence."*
What we don't want are these two scenarios, which I'm sure we all saw as students ourselves:

1. Teacher asks question. Students raise their hands. Teacher calls on a student with raised hand.
2. Student is inattentive. Teacher calls on the student to regain attention, or to punish them for not paying attention.

In recent studies, students who used imagery when learning vocabulary performed 37 percentage points higher than students who were just asked to continuously repeat the definition, and 21 percentage points higher than students who only used the new words in complete sentences (Marzano and Pickering, 2005). This is why it is important to have students create nonlinguistic definitions of the words. It might seem silly, especially in the upper grades, but it is a great technique to add to vocabulary instruction.

Vocabulary, like background knowledge, is needed to truly comprehend a topic or skill. Because of this, no matter the grade and no matter the subject, it is necessary that teachers explicitly teach vocabulary. Anita Archer, as well as other researchers, suggests teaching words that are necessary for the topic, but more importantly, words that the students will see again, especially in an academic setting. As a school team, grade-level team, or as an individual, educators can create a list of words important to teach. Another way to find key vocabulary is from predetermined word lists, like the Coxhead Academic Word List.

One way to create high standards for reading is to ask higher-order questions (see Bloom's Taxonomy). Studies have shown that by increasing the rigor of the comprehension questions, students will learn more and have a deeper understanding of literacy skills (Langer, 2001). This is easier said than done, but it's worth the effort. In order for students to develop a deep comprehension of complex text, they must access background knowledge on the subject, use reading strategies, and most importantly, think about what they are reading.

Research (Guthrie and Humenick, 2004) recommends that teachers try to:

1. Build student independence by allowing choices of texts and assignments;
2. Produce opportunities for students' social interactions focused on learning and understanding from text;
3. Ensure a variety of interesting texts are accessible to students; and
4. Focus students on significant and interesting learning goals.

As stated previously, it is crucial that teachers spend time on critical vocabulary terms and concepts, not just in the elementary grades but throughout. Studies have shown that vocabulary knowledge has a huge impact on the success of students as they progress through the grades (Stanovich, Cunningham, and Freeman, 1984). As terms taught in grade three help create the background knowledge for concepts learned in grade four, one can see the importance of making sure key concepts are mastered by all students.

Dr. Archer suggests the following strategies to increase vocabulary awareness while reading. This technique can be implemented throughout all content areas:

BEFORE READING THE PASSAGE

The teacher should introduce the pronunciation of words that are important to the passage and provide simple examples of meaning for these words.

The teacher should provide engaging instruction on selected vocabulary. These words should be words that are important to the topic, but also words that students will see again, even in other subjects. Asking students to find the definitions of words in a dictionary is *not* engaging. Studies have shown that around 60 percent of students incorrectly use a word if only a dictionary definition is given (Hatzivassiloglou and McKeown, 1993). Make sure any definitions provided are in student-friendly terms. Vocabulary can be learned using items like word maps, critical attribute templates, word diagrams, as well as other templates (sample templates are provided at the end of the book).

A word map (Schwartz, 1988; Schwartz & Raphael, 1985) is exactly what it sounds like: it is a map that shows the students an almost 360 degree look at the word. A word map usually has the vocabulary word in the middle of the template, a user-friendly definition, three items that are similar to the word, and three items examples of the word. For example, if the word was "large," a user-friendly definition could be "greater than average in size." Three items similar could be huge, big, and gigantic. Three examples could include an elephant, a skyscraper, and their father's pant size. The key to this is the student needs to create these examples, so the vocabulary word makes sense and connects to their prior knowledge (see figure 9.1).

A critical attribute template is another device that can be used to teach vocabulary. With a critical attribute template, the student writes down the vocabulary word as well as the part of speech to which the word belongs. Next, the student lists three to five critical attributes that define the vocabulary word. Finally, the student either writes the word in a sentence, draws an illustration, or provides examples of the word in the final column (see figure 9.2).

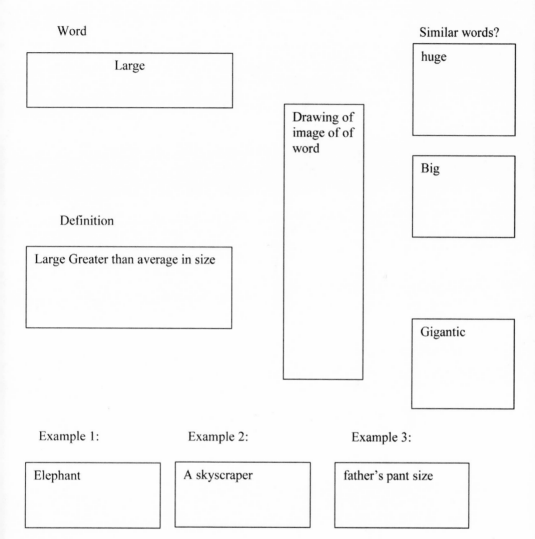

Word

Large

Similar words?

huge

Big

Gigantic

Drawing of
image of of
word

Definition

Large Greater than average in size

Example 1:

Elephant

Example 2:

A skyscraper

Example 3:

father's pant size

Figure 9.1

A word diagram is similar to a critical attribute template. With a word diagram, the student writes the word, the definition of the word, examples of what the word is like, and then non-examples (see figure 9.3).

Remember to teach or activate background knowledge. What are some items the students will already know about the subject? Try to tie in previously known information that is relevant to the new concept. If the students don't have the necessary background knowledge, teach a mini-lesson to help them get it.

Word and Part of Speech	Critical Attributes or Features	Sentence/Illustration/Examples
Texas noun	• Second largest state • Located in south central United States	

Figure 9.2

Word	Definition	Similar words or actions	Examples	Non-Examples
Implement	To put something into effect, or to carry something out	Starting something	Putting a plan into action	Just thinking about doing something

Figure 9.3 Word Diagrams Example

Also, assist the students in previewing the chapter. Previewing can be done by having the students read the headings and subheadings. This can assist the student in understanding the information that will be covered.

Lastly, help the students establish purpose for reading. Answer the question, "Why do we need to learn this?" before the students get the chance to ask it. Make sure there is a purpose for them to read the material.

DURING PASSAGE READING

Ask questions or have students generate questions. Generating questions about the reading helps students attend to the content, and self-check if it is being understood (Palincsar, Brown, and Campione, 1993). By asking questions, the students will self-engage themselves in the content.

Provide a study guide for use by the student or partners. A study guide will help the students work through the passage and understand where they are supposed to be and what they are supposed to learn.

Introduce strategies that students can utilize during reading, such as note taking skills, graphic organizers, and word or concept mapping. Some examples are provided at the end of the book.

AFTER PASSAGE READING

Assist the students in using or creating a graphic organizer to summarize the information they just read. Summarizing is a great skill that helps students retain important information.

Provide engaging vocabulary practice for selected words. The more times the students use the words, the more chances the teacher has to correct the usage, and the more times the student has to use the vocabulary and make it part of their repertoire.

Support students in completing assignments by presenting strategies to assist in the learning, and lastly, teach students how to write a summary. Ideally, this approach is done system wide, meaning every teacher, no matter the content, is doing it.

Studies on the characteristics of effective vocabulary instruction (Marzano and Pickering, 2005) confirm this approach:

1. Effective vocabulary instruction does not rely on definitions
2. Students must represent their knowledge of words in linguistic and non-linguistic ways
3. Effective vocabulary instruction involves the gradual shaping of word meanings through multiple exposures
4. Teaching word parts enhances students' understanding of terms
5. Different types of words require different types of instruction
6. Students should discuss the terms they are learning
7. Students should play with words
8. Instruction should focus on terms that have a high probability of enhancing academic success

REFLECTION SCENARIO

You peek your head into your next door teacher's classroom to see if she will cover your classroom so you can take a quick restroom break. She is in the middle of a vocabulary lesson. You hear her say the next word is "countenance." Who knows what countenance means? Rachel?" Rachel says, "Doesn't it mean like counting in a certain way?" The teacher replies, "No, that's not quite it. Does anyone else have an idea what countenance means?" Juan's hand goes up. The teacher calls on Juan and he offers, "I think it means some kind of emotion." The teacher responds, "You're getting closer." This drags on another five minutes until she asks someone to look up the word. Many experts refer to this as a "fishing expedition" and caution that students will retain the first often incorrect meaning offered. Many of us are guilty of using this method one time or another. In what ways do you see this detrimental to the vocabulary process and instruction? Apply some of the strategies mentioned in this chapter to rewrite the scenario. What are some ways explicit vocabulary instruction would impact your classroom?

Chapter 10

Did They Learn It? What Evidence Do You Have?

> Without question . . . students must be regarded as the most important users of classroom assessment results.
>
> —Richard J. Stiggins

When a group of educators get together, or when an educator gets together with an adult that has kids in school, the conversation eventually turns to assessment and standardized testing. Unfortunately there seems to be a misconception of the word *assessment*. Many educators interpret assessment to mean standardized testing; however assessment is so much more. Assessment is truly a part of the minute-to-minute, day-to-day teaching and learning in the classroom. Some type of assessment needs to take place so that teachers truly know if students have learned information. Assessment provides us with evidence regarding the extent to which the student understands a concept as well as how well the teacher taught the concept and what adjustments the teacher might need to make in their teaching to accommodate the varying needs of students.

Remember, a teacher's job is to assist students to obtain new knowledge and skills and apply the new learning in other situations.

Examples of Knowledge (what students should know):

- Vocabulary
- Terminology
- Definitions
- Facts
- Locations
- Details
- Events/people
- Timeline

Examples of Skills (what we want students to be able to do):

- Decoding
- Computations
- Listening, speaking, writing
- Compare, infer, analyze, interpret
- Inquiry, investigations
- Note taking, outlines
- Work with groups

A teacher cannot know if a student has obtained this new knowledge or skill without giving some sort of assessment.

A good definition for assessment is the information you receive from the student that provides evidence of their learning. Assessment can occur in the beginning of a lesson to see what the students already know (pre-assessment), informally throughout the lesson (formative assessment) or at the end in order to provide a grade or score (summative assessment), (Guskey, 2003).

There are many different types of assessments, and they all have different purposes, and can happen at different times with different frequencies. This is called a balanced assessment system. For example, figure 10.1 shows what a balanced assessment system could look like.

Please note that as in any balanced assessment system, each type of assessment has a purpose and expectations of use. These expectations can vary depending if the user is the teacher, the student, the principal, or the district.

So what type of assessments should teachers use? Before answering that question, teachers should refer to three key principles: consider albums versus snapshots, the measurement must match the goal, and form follows function (Forster and Masters, 2004).

CONSIDER PHOTO ALBUMS VERSUS SNAPSHOTS

Dependable assessments that demand multiple sources of evidence are more reliable than "one shot" snapshots. A variety of classroom assessments can show a teacher and the student if any progress has been made throughout the unit, week, or even semester. A variety of assessments is important from a measurement perspective, but also as a matter of sensitivity to varied learners.

Table 10.1. Sample Balanced Assessment Framework

Assessment Cycle	Assessment Type	Assessment Tool	Student Use Expectations	Teacher Use Expectations
Constant or Daily	Formative classroom assessments. Embedded in teacher instruction.	Questioning techniques. Formative Assessment practices, such as white boards, check for understanding, exit tickets, whip-arounds, etc. Planned interactions.	Self-monitored understanding of the learning targets.	Check for student understanding. Revise instruction or re-teach if needed. Use formative assessment data to decide how to move forward with the instruction and learning. Provide feedback to students.
Weekly or Monthly	Formative classroom assessments. Could be "common formative assessments" done by grade level.	Weekly or monthly assessments to inform instruction, such as work samples, journals, performance tasks, essential questions, etc.	Check progress of learning target.	Check for student understanding. Revise instruction or re-teach if needed. Provide feedback to students. Identify students who need targeted interventions.
Unit	Unit testing	End of unit or end of chapter tests	Gauge progress toward meeting grade-level standards.	Assign grades. Provide feedback to students. Further identify students who need targeted interventions.
Quarterly	Quarterly assessments Benchmark testing Interim testing	District created benchmarks, or commercial benchmarking software such as: Galileo, ATI, NWEA, etc.	Gauge progress toward meeting grade-level standards.	Assign grades. Provide feedback to students. Identify which students need additional interventions.
Annual	End-of-year testing	State test, national test, and international test.	Gauge if grade level standards have been met.	Identify which students need additional interventions.

(Based on a model created by the Syracuse City School District and New York Comprehensive Center)

THE MEASURES MUST MATCH WITH THE GOALS

Don't keep your assessments secret. Let the students know what you will be assessing. The assessment should be on what was taught, and the important stuff that was taught, not obscure facts or something that was only mentioned for one second. An assessment must provide an appropriate measure of a given goal. Basically, there are three types of educational goals:

- Declarative knowledge (knowing, who, what, where, when, why)
- Procedural knowledge (knowing how to do something, or a procedure)
- Dispositions (attitudes or beliefs)

Bear in mind that there is a difference between *knowing* (either you know it or don't) and *understanding* (matter of degree one can explain, interpret, apply, have perspective, display empathy, and show meta-cognitive awareness). For evidence of knowing in an assessment, remember the GRASPS acronym (Wiggins and McTighe, 1999):

Goal: "Your task or goal is to create/write . . ."

Role: Example: "Approach this as though you are a . . ." "Make believe that you are a _____, and create it from that point of view."

Audience: "Your audience is. . . ."

Situation: "Your challenge is to take this point of view . . ." "Your challenge is to use only these materials . . ."

Product/performance: Example: "You will create a . . ." You will write a . . ."

Standards: "Your performance needs to meet these criteria . . ."

FORM FOLLOWS FUNCTION

Design and use of classroom assessments should be influenced by three questions: What is being assessed, why is it being assessed, and how will the results be used and by whom? Start with the end in mind. Based on the standards, what do you want the students to know and be able to do? Let this guide your teaching.

TYPES OF ASSESSMENTS

Not all assessments are used the same, and the goals of these assessments vary as well (Heritage, Vendlinski, and Herman, 2009).

Summative assessments are given at a specific time to show what a student does or doesn't know. The most common summative assessment is the end of chapter test, or the end of year exam. This type of assessment is often graded and used for accountability. Summative assessments necessitate the application of skills, concepts, and understandings.

Formative assessments take place during the teaching or during the student practice to determine how well the learning objectives are being met. These are mostly observational in style, but can also take place in short quizzes or other means. These assessments let the teacher know if they need to slow down the pace of the course, or if they need to address the material in a different fashion.

Formative assessments help teachers modify instruction, and help the teachers decide when the topic is clearly understood and future instruction can follow. Teachers can use this information to make necessary instructional changes, including reteaching, alternative instructional practices, or as simple as spending more time on a topic (Heritage, Vendlinski, and Herman, 2009). The purpose of formative assessments is to make immediate changes so the learning is taking place and the student is keeping pace, so eventually the student can pass the summative assessment.

Pre-assessments (also called *diagnostic assessments*) are used to assess prior knowledge. These types of assessments are given before a new unit or course as a baseline of what knowledge students are bringing with them. These types of assessments should never be graded, and the results should be used to address concepts that will be needed for the new material to truly be learned (Wiggins, 1998).

Now that we've covered the different types of assessments, how should they be used in a classroom?

All good teachers should assess their class before they start teaching. A solid pre-assessment will focus on the essential knowledge of the unit, and should not be graded (McMillan, 2000). The pre-assessment will assist the teacher in determining what needs to be taught, as well as what concepts or misconceptions the students are already bringing to the learning.

When assessing knowledge or skills, if possible, choices should be provided to the class (Kellough and Kellough, 1999). Students should be given the chance to work to their strengths or have an option on how they will demonstrate the knowledge, skill, or understanding to the teacher. If the teacher provides a list of evidence needed from the student to show mastery of a concept, why not let the student decide in which form the evidence will be provided? The use of an evaluative criteria rubric can provide this information to the student. Any rubric criteria must be based on the goal of the learning or content (rubrics are discussed in more detail toward the end of this chapter).

The reason to assess is to get data on what the student knows. Planning to succeed as a teacher relies on the use of data as the key to continuous improvement. When using data to provide focus for your improvements, patterns within the data will create targets or a pathway for your instructional strategies, as well as the effectiveness of those strategies. By reflecting on data, an educator can see trends in the feedback and decide to "stay the course" or refine their approach.

There are four types that can be used as indicators of school or district success: achievement data, demographic data, program data, and perception data (Bernhardt, 2004). This book will focus on achievement data.

Achievement data educators can use to guide instruction comes in three forms (Learning Point Associates, 2004).

Annual, Large-Scale Assessment Data. This type of data is designed primarily for accountability purposes, such as the annual state testing, and provides a summative snapshot of a student's strengths and weaknesses.

Periodic Assessment Data. Given throughout the school year at specific times, periodic assessments, sometimes called "benchmark tests," can provide immediate results of student performance on key standards-based skills in a content area and grade level. These should be given when the school year begins, and by continuing to use these assessments throughout the year, teachers and administrators can assist in tracking students' progress and their strengths and weaknesses in particular content areas.

These types of assessments can assist in grouping students based on their changing skill needs and which students need interventions. Periodic assessments can also inform teachers of what content might need to be retaught. Content area teams or cross-content teams can also use this data to see what information students have learned, and what topics need to continue to be addressed.

Ongoing Classroom Assessment Data. This type of formative data is focused on the individual classroom. This tells the teacher is the students are "getting" it, and can assist the teacher in moving from the "I do" part of instruction to the "we do" and "you do." This "on-the-spot" assessment informs the educator about student understanding at a point when timely adjustments can be made to the lesson.

When looking at achievement data, the educator should ask themselves what information can be gleaned, such as: What evidence do we have that shows the knowledge, skills, and understandings our students have achieved? Which data indicate the degree to which our students show the conceptual understandings and generalizations in our standards? What evidence shows which students are meeting or exceeding our achievement expectations and which are not? What do we know about how each individual student learns?

Research suggests that teachers should use an assessment blueprint to ensure that the assessment offers a broad range of thinking, including

Table 10.2. Bloom's Chart

Dimension	Definition	Examples
Remember	*Promoting retention of the presented material in much time the same form as it was taught*	
Recognizing	Locating knowledge in long-term memory is consistent with presented material	The attack on Pearl Harbor occurred in 1941. True or False How many sides does a triangle have? A)1 B) 2 C)3
Recalling	Recalling relevant knowledge from long term memory when given a prompt to so do	On what date did the attack on Pearl Harbor occur? How many sides does a triangle have?
Understand	*Construct meaning from instructional messages, including oral, written, and graphic communication*	
Interpreting	Converting information from one representational form to another	Draw a picture of the checks and balances system in government. Explain in your own words how the system works.
Exemplifying	Give specific examples, an instance of defining the features of a general concept or principle	Give an example of a dangling modifier.
Classifying	Recognizing that something belongs to a certain category or detecting relevant features/patterns that fit the concept or principle.	Which of the following is a mammal: crow, salmon, bacteria Sort the following numbers based on if they are a polynomial or a monomial.
Summarizing	Suggesting a single statement that represents information or abstracts a general theme.	Write a statement summarizing the plot of the story "The Necklace."
Inferring	Finding a pattern within a series of examples and inducing a pattern based on given information or a series of examples	Based on this series: 3, 6, 12, 24 what number do you think comes next? Based on the end of chapter 3, what do you predict will happen in chapter 4?

(continued)

Table 10.2.   Bloom's Chart *(continued)*

Dimension	*Definition*	*Examples*
Comparing	Detecting similarities and differences between two or more objects, events, ideas, problems, or situations.	Tell how the two experiments were alike and different. Using the diagram, explain the similarities and differences between the Catholic and Mormon religions.
Explaining	Constructing and/or using a cause-effect model of a system	Explain how a liquid becomes a gas.
Apply	*Using procedures to perform exercises or solve problems*	
Executing	Carrying out a procedure when given a familiar task/exercise	Using the taught procedure, execute an effective bench press. Using the Pythagorean theorem . . .
Implementing	Selecting and using a procedure to perform an unfamiliar task/exercise	Solve the following word problem.
Analyze	*Breaking materials into its constituent parts and determining how the parts are related to one another and to an overall structure.*	
Differentiating	Distinguishing the parts of a whole structure in terms of their relevance or importance.	Read the following story and decide which information is relevant or not relevant.
Organizing	Building systematic and coherent connections among pieces of information.	Prepare an outline for your report.
Attributing	Ability to ascertain the point of view, biases, values or intention underlying communication.	What do you think was the purpose of this editorial?
Evaluate	*Making judgments based on clearly defined criteria and standards.*	

Table 10.2. Bloom's Chart *(continued)*

Dimension	Definition	Examples
Checking	Involves testing for internal inconsistencies or fallacies	What are possible problems with Marxism? Based on the argument, what inconsistencies were made?
Critiquing	Judging a product or operation based on externally imposed criteria and standards	Based on the 6 Traits Scoring Rubric, score the following paper on conventions and organization.
Create	*Putting elements together to form a coherent or functional whole. It may or may not include originality or uniqueness. It is drawing upon elements from many sources and putting them together into a structure or pattern relative to one's own prior knowledge.*	
Generating	Redefining, arriving at alternatives or hypothesis that meet certain criteria.	List plausible alternatives to gasoline as a fuel.
Planning	Developing a solution method when given a problem.	List the steps you will use to correctly build a functional kitchen cabinet system.
Producing	Carrying out a plan for solving a given problem that meets certain specifications,	Build a functional kitchen cabinet system.

higher-order thinking (Brookhart, 2010). This example in Table 10.2 provides the content, or topic being assessed, as well as the cognitive domain of Bloom' revised taxonomy (Anderson, Krathwohl, Airasain, Cruikshank, Mayer, Pintrich, Raths and Wittrock, 2001). This allows the teacher to map out the assessment and check to make sure more than one domain is being assessed.

As a beginning teacher, the assessment map can make creating assessments easier. After a while, you will begin to remember which verbs (define, identify, distinguish, etc.) belong to which cognitive domain, and the use of the assessment map might become more infrequent.

Once an assessment is created, make sure to look over the test and check to see if anything is confusing or unclear. Can anything be misinterpreted?

Once the test results are given, then what? How will the teacher provide corrective instruction to ensure the students know what they missed, what the correct answer is, and why? Margaret Heritage, author and vocal supporter of formative assessment, states that this is "a process that is fundamental and indigenous to the practice of teaching and learning." (Heritage, 2010). Formative assessment provides the *adjustments* teachers make in response to evidence (blank stares, wrong answers, the look of confusion), the *feedback* teachers give students in response to evidence (their work or product), and the student's *self-assessment* based on evidence (the student saying "I get this, but not that," or using a rubric to rate their own work so the teacher can adjust the teaching and learning). The key word is evidence. The teacher is continuously looking for immediate evidence that the students are learning, and the teacher is adjusting instruction based on the evidence.

There are four essential elements to the formative assessment process (Heritage, 2010):

1. Identifying the gap between where students are and where they should be, as well as what instruction will help close the gap.
2. Providing feedback—in the formative assessment realm, this feedback should be a constant exchange between the student and teacher. The conversation of where the learning is must take place.
3. Increasing active engagement—the students must be engaged to let you know what they know or don't know.
4. Creating progressions in learning. There need to be checks within the progress of the learning to make sure the students are with you, or when some students are starting to fall behind. This will assist the teacher when helping those students.

Many people—and this is backed by research—confuse formative assessment with interim assessments (Perie, Marion, and Gong, 2009). As stated earlier in the book, interim assessments, also called benchmark assessments, are planned assessments throughout the year (usually quarterly) that benchmark where a student is in regard to the content they are expected to know at the year's end. Interim assessments, like summative assessments, are an instrument used to see where a student is academically (Stiggins, 2008). Most likely, if your school or district says they have "purchased a formative assessment program," in reality bought an interim assessment program.

Formative assessment makes more sense if you think of it as "formative instruction"; unlike a product or instrument that is administered, formative assessment guides the real-time adjustments or processes a teacher makes while instructing a class to ensure that the students are learning the content or skill (Heritage, 2010). These adjustments can be as simple as restating a fact, speaking slower, repeating an answer, or modeling a skill one more time. It can be as complex as taking a completely different approach to the concept, creating small group teams for those that are struggling, or providing explicit feedback as to what the student is doing right or wrong.

Formative feedback needs to meet a couple of criteria (Hattie and Timperely, 2007). One, it needs to be precise and directly help the student correct the mistake or perform the skill correctly. As stated earlier, the terms "good job" or "nope, it's still wrong" are *not* formative feedback.

Two, effective feedback needs to guide or offer the student a way confirming their performance or ways to increase the performance. For example, a teacher might say, *"Tell me how you thought through this problem of dividing your half of the pizza into equal pieces to feed three more people. Think about the entire pizza.* (using manipulatives fraction pieces) *If you divided the other half of pizza just like this one, how many pieces would you have? That's right three more pieces. So how many pieces would be in the entire pizza? That's right, 6 altogether. So when you had a ½ divided by 3 they would only have 1/6 of the entire pizza to each eat."*

Effective formative feedback should provide enough information for the student to understand where they are and where they need to be, as well as how to get there. With the use of feedback, the student can place new information with schemata formed by previous knowledge, and therefore make the connections needed to learn the new skill or concept. Good teachers provide feedback frequently and make sure the feedback is specific to the skills of the student. Feedback must be provided in a timely manner and must state specifically what the student did right as well as how they can improve (Heritage, 2010). Marking a paper "good" or "needs improvement" is *not* specific feedback. The student should be able to read the comments and understand what need improvement, or understand what was specifically done correct. *Feedback is an essential way to increase student learning and provide the student with the knowledge needed to improve performance.*

Feedback needs to focus on something with a purpose and with significance. As educators we have limited time with our students, and need to use this time wisely. Because of this, when dialoging with students about their performance, focus on things that count and things that they can replicate in the future (Black and Wiliam, 1998).

Feedback should not be stated as a judgment. It should be consistent, and it should be based on some form of evaluation. Feedback needs to be specific, and be presented objectively. Make sure that you are pointing out what the student did right was well as what the student can improve. For students that are struggling or don't seem attached to school, try to point out more things they did correct at first to show them that although they are struggling, they are making gains as well. After pointing out the correct items, provide students with areas in which they can improve and show them what they can do to improve. If effective feedback has been provided, students should know exactly how to make the product better.

Feedback also consists of the teacher speaking as well as listening. For example, after providing specific guidance as to how a student can improve the closing paragraph by restating the opening thesis in a different manner, the student might reply in a way that lets the teacher know the student truly doesn't understand. If the teacher isn't listening, if the teacher is only talking and not letting the student respond, then this teachable moment will not be presented. As with any relationship, it is *key* to listen. The relationship between the teacher and the student is no different.

Remember, when providing feedback, it is important to reinforce the good as well as provide ways for refinement. When reinforcing the good:

- Restate the objective or purpose of the assignment.
- Give clear and specific examples from the assignment where the student achieved the objective or purpose of the assignment.
- Reinforce the student achievement by explaining exactly why sections of the assignment or skill met the objective of the lesson.

When providing ways for refinement (that's a nice way of saying improvement):

- Prioritize the areas of refinement that are most important. Make sure to only focus on one or two areas of refinement. Focusing on too many areas of refinement can cause the student to lose faith in their ability to achieve the required result.
- Restate the objective or purpose of the assignment.
- Provide clear evidence as to why the area of refinement does not meet the objective.
- Provide clear examples of how the student can make the area of refinement meet the objective.
- Provide an opportunity for the student to refine the area, or have the student say in their own words how they could improve the area of refinement in future assignments.

The last key part of formative assessment is empowering students to assess their own work, or assess how well they understand something. The authors have heard experts refer to this as creating a culture where it is okay to make a mistake. Often this takes a teacher strong enough to admit his mistakes and show students how the teacher has learned from the mistake. This is harder than it sounds. By asking a student to assess what they know, the teachers needs to (A) create a safe classroom atmosphere where a student knows her admission of not knowing something will only be used to help them learn it, not to be scored and decrease a grade; and (B) show the students what they are supposed to know, or help them understand what the exemplary product should look like (Heritage, 2010).

For the first part, if a student feels that "if I say I don't get it, I'll get an F" there is no way the student will be open about where they are in the learning. The teacher needs to explain that the purpose of self-assessment is for the teacher to help, and these self-assessments will never be graded. Second, the teacher needs to help the student understand the final product or skill level so the student knows if he is at an appropriate level of understanding. This can best be done with rubrics, exemplars, or good samples of previous student work. Good teachers let students reflect on their own work, and provide the students will a self-assessment rubric or reflective questions to help guide the student in their thinking (Bandura, 1997).

Formative assessment is only as good as the feedback that accompanies it. Formative assessment is really formative learning or formative teaching. If the teacher uses the "real time data" during the instructional process to change instruction and adapt the teaching, then the teacher has formatively assessed the class and changed the learning. Planning for formative assessment begins as soon as the teacher begins deciding on the learning goals and what would be considered evidence of success for those learning goals.

The evidence of the learning can be from active engagement strategies, and even as simple as thumbs up or down, lesson checks, notes to teachers, and so forth. Based on the student's reaction or answers, the teacher determines if the students are ready for more information, or what they haven't acquired and need more support with.

The teacher can then provide feedback based on the evidence, and try to close the knowledge gap.

Because the teacher has to close the knowledge gap, the teacher will modify instruction, or create a new plan for the learning. The teacher can break the learning into smaller increments to scaffold the learning for the students. Once the gap is closed, the process begins again.

Seeing that five students in your class do not understand generic rectangles is important, but the feedback you provide, the intervention to offset their lack of comprehension, is where the magic of formative assessment lays. One simple way of providing feedback is to discuss the mistake, making sure the student observes what was done correctly. Another way is to compare the student answer to the correct answer, and discuss with the student where the mistake was made, and more importantly, what needs to be done to make the answer correct. Prompt the student, "So walk me through: how you did this . . ." and provide the correction when they hit the misstep. This can also be done to etch the correct answer, "This is perfect. Tell me how you got this done . . ." The feedback needs to be clear enough so the student can tell exactly where the error lies, and exactly what was done right—what not to change and what to continue to reproduce.

SUMMATIVE ASSESSMENT

Even with summative assessments, we want to take the "luck" out of the assessment outcome. For example, most multiple choice questions have four answers. This means if a student gets the answer correct, is it because the student knew the answer, or is it that the student guessed and got lucky? In a four-answer multiple choice question, there is a 25 percent chance the student could get the answer right without knowing the answer. One way to get around this is to require the students write a sentence or two about how they knew the answer was correct, or in mathematics, have the students show their work. By doing this, the teacher can compare the multiple choice answer with the student thought process and decide if luck was involved.

Essay questions are another good way of ensuring whether a student truly knows the answer. The caution is some students are better writers than others, and a poor essay response due to limited writing skills can downplay what a student actually knows, while vivid and rich writing skills can mask misunderstanding. Also, if as a teacher you rely on essay questions, make sure you use a rubric to grade them, therefore allowing the students to know what it is you expect for full points and to also ensure you are scoring all fair and objectively.

As any honest teacher will admit, if you are grading 40–50 essay questions and not using a rubric, there is a great chance that as grading becomes cumbersome, the overall scores will either decline or increase, and if the last essay score you graded is held next to the first you graded two hours ago, there could be inconsistencies on the teacher's part.

Now that you understand the different purposes of assessments, let's spend a minute and talk about what classroom assessments can *look* like. Think of the term "classroom assessment." What comes to mind? For many it might be completing worksheets or writing extended essays. Although these are types of assessments, there are so many more items to add to your repertoire. But before you decide to create a classroom assessment, make sure to ask yourself, "How will this assessment inform me of my teaching and my students' learning?" "What am I trying to assess?" We should have a clear understanding or target of the expectation. What do want the students to know and be able to do?

It could be that we just want to target the student's *knowledge* or recall, for example, "name the capital of New Mexico."

It could be that we want to target the student's *reasoning*: "If two trains are heading to Texas and one is going 50 mph, and then other is going 75mph . . ."

It could be that we want to target the student's *performance*: "Run one mile in under nine minutes."

It could be that we want to target the student's development of a *product*: "Cook a chocolate cake using the eight-step recipe we learned this week."

In order to have a clear target, we need to take three things into consideration (Smaldino, Lowther, and Russell, 2007):

Conditions: define the materials available. "After reading the story *Othello* . . ."

Behavior: what will the student do? This has a verb: solve, compare, etc.

Criterion or Degree: how will we know if it is achieved? What will we measure?

Once we take the conditions, behavior, and criterion into consideration, we can have a clear target, for example, "After reading the play *Othello*, the student will compare three the character traits of Iago and Othello."

Assessment items like true or false, fill-in-the-blank, and multiple choice are good to use if you only want the students to recall information or identify facts or concepts. These items are called *select response items*. With select response times, each question has a right and wrong answer and can be impartially scored. It is important to note from Blooms Taxonomy which cognitive level is being addressed; you do not want all the questions to be at the lower-level of thinking skills.

Select response items are usually pretty easy for a teacher to create, and can often be used year after year. The drawback to these items is they aren't very engaging, can often be seen as busy work, can often provide incorrect data (what if the kid picked the right true or false answer by luck, not by knowledge?), and aren't process based (they are based on content.) Items like these are fine to use in moderation, but don't fall into the trap of handing out worksheets everyday to your class.

When using multiple choice, up the ante by offering "distracters." Distracters are wrong answers that look like they could be right, and can also be used to inform a teacher as to what the student doesn't understand. For example, let's look at this simple mathematics problem:

2 + 5 x 2 = ?

A) 12
B) 14
C) 9
D) 11

The correct answer is A, 12. Based on the distracters, if a student answered B, the teacher would know the student made an order of operations mistake and added 2 +5 first and then multiplied by 2. If the student answered C, the teacher could assume the student added all the numbers and didn't multiply. By making sure that at least two or more options are incorrect within reason, the teacher can use the data to correct the student's mistake. If the other wrong answer options were unrealistic, like (A) 12, (B) 2000, (C) 0, (D) 1,000,001, the teacher would have no way of assessing the student's mistake.

When writing a multiple choice question, make sure all the answers seem like they could be the correct answer, and make sure they are homogenous, or the answers should seem at first glance like possible answers, and all answers should be similarly grouped. Answers should also be similar in length and grammatical form (Florida Center for Instructional Technology).

For example: The third president of the United States was:

A) Abraham Lincoln
B) Thomas Jefferson
C) Andrew Jackson
D) James Monroe

As you can see, all the choices are presidents and they all served within the first 10 terms. All the answers are similar in length.

Here's a non-example: The third president of the United States was:

E) Bart Simpson
F) Thomas Jefferson
G) President and Army General Andrew Jackson
H) LeBron James

In this example, only two are plausible answers, and the group is not homogenous (two are presidents, one is a basketball player, and one is a cartoon character). All the answers are also not similar in length.

When creating a matching question, the same rules for the multiple choice questions apply. Make sure the answers are homogenous, similar in length and similar in grammatical form. Some teachers like to add more answers than questions, but this is really up to the teacher's discretion. Having more answers than questions does increase the change that the student knows the correct answer and wasn't just using the process of elimination.

If you are writing a true or false statement within an assessment, ensure the statement is completely true or completely false. If they aren't, you will confuse the students, so make sure the statement is clear and not confusing. Try not to use "always" or "never." These words are dead giveaways that the answer is probably false.

Here's an example: True or False: Andrew Jackson vetoed the renewal of the national bank charter (True).

In this example; the statement is completely true and is clear.

Here's a non-example: True or False: Andrew Jackson always vetoed anything that had to do with national rights over states rights because states right allowed for him to extend his wealth.

This non-example is confusing and is not completely true. Jackson was pro-states rights, but the reasons varied, and a historian could most likely find an instance where he didn't veto a measure that supported national power.

Another type of assessment is the *open response assessment*, also called the constructed response assessment. These might provide a sentence stem, or pose a question, and will offer many different forms of responses. These types of assessments make the student process information, interpret their learning, and provide reasoning behind their answers. These take longer to grade than the closed task assessment mentioned above, but they do provide more evidence of what the child really learned. An essay or extended response would fall under this category. Some example of open response questions could be:

The Industrial Revolution had a deep effect on human history. In your opinion, what was the most important innovation during this time? Explain why you think it had the biggest impact on this time period.

The Women's Rights Movement had an impact on America by . . .

Fill-in-the-blank questions are probably the most common constructed response item used in education. If you are creating a fill-in-the-blank question, make sure the question has a definite answer, and only have one blank per item.

For example: The third president of the United States was: ＿＿＿＿＿.

In this example, there is only one correct answer, Thomas Jefferson.

Here is a non-example: The ＿＿＿＿ of the ＿＿＿＿＿ was ＿＿＿＿＿.

In this non-example, based on the number of blanks, many different sentences could be completed that may be a correct statement, although not the one the teacher was looking for.

Essays are a much deeper type of constructed response assessment. A prompt for an essay question should explain exactly how a student is to respond and should emphasize higher-level thinking.

For example: Based on three current news articles, create an exit plan for the United States to leave in Iraq. Include political, military, and economic solutions.

In this example, the students are told specifically what to focus on, and the essay prompt emphasizes more than just recall of facts.

Here's a non-example: Write about getting the United States out of Iraq.

In this non-example, the poorly-written essay prompt is vague and leaves a lot to be desired.

Performance tasks are a great way for students to show procedural knowledge. With a performance task, the student actually does something. For example, *"Show me how to clean a carburetor." "Use the scientific method to solve . . ."*

Journals are another way to assess what a student knows. Journals can be used by having students write about what they know about a topic before and after a lesson to show growth, or can be used to summarize their learning for the lesson. Based on the entries, the teacher can see what the students retained, as well as any misinformation they might have.

A student-to-teacher interview can be used as an assessment. Although time consuming, these provide an open conversation about learning and can bring a lot to the table. In these academic interviews, the teach sits down with an individual student and asks specific questions about a certain subject. For example, "We've been talking about plot lately. What can you tell me about the plot of *Romeo and Juliet*?"

A good assessment will allow the teacher to see where the student went wrong; where the student needs more help or assistance. By analyzing the assessments, teachers can tell what the students learned, as well as what areas need to be retaught. Remember—reteaching doesn't mean teaching the content in the same way as previously done. Corrective teaching needs to be systematic and direct. After it is retaught, *the student should have the opportunity to retest and improve the grade.*

If we as educators want children to actually enjoy learning, we have to show them that it isn't a do-or-die situation where they will learn to fear and hate learning. We have to show them that their education is what matters to us, and if they show us they don't know something (which is the purest sense to give an assessment) we will help them learn it and show us that they know it. *The key is to educate all children, not just the children who got it right the first time around.*

A *reliable* assessment means that if you give the assessment five times, it should consistently show what the student does or does not know. In other words, a student should not be able to get a 90 percent on a test, and then take it again and get a 60 percent if the test is reliable.

A *valid* assessment means the assessment measures what it is supposed to be measuring. This means it is measuring the skills that the student was taught. For example, if you are learning how to make frosting for a cake, an assessment should not be asking you to cook a chicken. In a less extreme analogy, if the teacher is teaching sentence combining, the assessment should be on sentence combining, not dangling modifiers.

When discussing validity, the subject is usually separated into three types: content validity, criterion validity, and construct validity (Dulewicz, Higgs, Slaski, 2003).

Content validity asks the question "does the test match the instructional objectives?" Does the test match what was taught? The frosting-chicken analogy would be an example of poor content validity.

Criterion validity asks the question "do the scores align with other criteria?" For example, if the student aces your class algebra test, is there a great chance the student will also pass the state algebra test, or a national algebra test? Criterion validity means that the assessment scores will correlate with a similar score from another similar assessment.

Construct validity asks the question "does the assessment measure the construct (or concept) it is supposed to be measuring?" Basically, does the test make the concept into something that is functional?

GRADING

In many classrooms and schools across the country, grading is pretty much the professional judgment call on the part of the teacher (Guskey, 2000). What do we mean by this? Basically, if it is up to the teacher to decide what constitutes an "A," "B," "C," "D," or "F," then the grade is based on the opinion (and hopefully the professional opinion) of the individual teacher. Do the students know how they will be assessed? Have you clarified for the students what the criteria is for an "A," "B," "C," "D," or "F"? Have you shown students an example of an "A" paper as well as an example of a failing paper? If another teacher walked into the room, could she tell what is being assessed? Is the assessment good or reliable? Does it truly show what the student knows?

Does it somehow benefit one type or race of student? Is the product indicative of what the student really knows?

Students shouldn't be surprised by the assessment—it should be a natural way for them to show what they know based on what was taught. According to Thomas Guskey, "Assessments reflect the concepts and skills that the teacher emphasized in class, along with the teacher's clear criteria for judging students' performance" (2003).

Hopefully the teacher has determined the criteria he is looking for within each grade mark and is holding all student work to the same level of those criteria. Before we continue, ask yourself this question: What is the purpose of grading? The authors bet that if you go to your school and ask that question to all the teachers and administrators, there is a good chance there will be many answers.

Although all teachers tend to grade something, rarely do we talk to each other about its purpose. Grading seems to be one of those things we never question in the field of education; it has been handed down to us by the elders of our profession so we do it without ever asking "why do we do this? Are we all on the same page? Are we all basing our grades on the same factors?"

For example, if a student shows up everyday, always turns in homework, but gets "Cs" on all the tests, what is the highest grade he can receive in your class? The answer isn't as important as the justification of the answer. If you say they can still get an "A," then what criteria for the "A" do you as the teacher need to see? How do you know the student understands the concepts and skills they are expected to know? If you say "C" then do the students in your class understand that even if they show up and do all the homework, they can only get as high of a grade as what they get on formal exams?

Another question could be if a student gets an "A" on every test, but continuously is confrontational with the teacher, what is the highest grade the student could get? Is the student there to learn and show their academic prowess, or is the student there to listen and respect the teacher? Again, the answer is not as important as your justification for the answer.

During Oran's first year as a teacher, grading seemed to be something that piled up and he'd find himself grading papers while eating dinner or grading papers while watching television. He never thought twice about doing this until he had his first parent-teacher conference. The conference was for a student who was getting a "D" in his class, and they endlessly butted heads during class. Well, his parents were not happy—with Oran! For an hour he had to justify the grades he had given this student, as well as explain how the student fared compared to other students in the class. Could Oran prove that the student's grade was based on his performance, and not the sour relationship? Oran second-guessed how he graded after that conference because one thing became apparent: he did not have a way of ensuring that he graded all the papers the same way with the same expectations, and when asked, he couldn't provide a set of criteria to justify his grading system. If he gave a paper an "A," and if it was snuck back into his grading pile, could he ensure that he'd give it an "A" again, and based on the same criteria? If someone randomly placed an "A" paper and a "B" paper in front of him, could he state the differences to justify the difference in grades? From that day on Oran took grading more seriously and searched for a more systematic way of doing it.

When it comes to grading or scoring, two types of grading approaches are often mentioned: norm-referenced grading and criteria-referenced grading (Bond, 1996). Norm-referenced grading compares a student's performance to the performance of other students within the class. This creates a rank within the class and then shows where that student is within that rank order. For example, "Johnny did better than 75 percent of his class." Norm-referenced grading also creates the bell curve, which is how many of us were graded when we were in school. Based on norm-referenced grading and the bell curve, only about 16 percent of the students will get an "A," 34 percent a "B," 34 percent a "C," 16 percent a "D" or an "F."

Now, although knowing where a child is in reference to the rest of his class is important, the problem with norm-referenced grading and the bell curve is this: Some students are forced to get an F, even if they know the material, but just not as well as their classmates. To further develop this topic, take the following scenario: Judy is a 4th grade student who takes a math test. Twenty problems are possible. Judy completes 14 problems correctly. Based on the 14 problems correctly answered, it is clear that Judy does understand the skills that meet the performance objective for her grade level. There are 10 students in Judy's class. The rest of the students scored accordingly: 20, 20, 19, 18, 18, 17, 17, 16, and 16. Based on the bell curve, even though Judy got 70 percent of the questions correct, Judy is in the bottom percentile in her class. And, technically based on the bell curve, the bottom 16 percent must receive a "D" or an "F."

Now, hopefully a teacher using norm-referenced testing would understand that in this situation the bell curve should not apply. Even though a teacher could still rank all students, there's no way to justify failing a student that has shown the abilities required within her grade level even though her "high-flying" classmates might have done better. On the opposite side of the spectrum, a student could get an "A" on a test for having the highest score in the class, although the student really didn't demonstrate mastery of a concept, he did better than the rest of the class. Also, because the highest scoring student dictates what grades the other students will get, some students can be ostracized for being the smartest student in the class, therefore setting a tone that there's something wrong with being intelligent. An alternative to this is to use criterion-referenced grading.

Criterion-referenced grading is what it sounds like: a student gets scored based on what criteria they complete. The criteria are based on performance objectives the student is expected to learn at that grade level. In this system of grading, if all the students meet the criteria for the grade of an "A," then all the students would receive an "A." The perks of this system are multiple:

1. Students are not competing against each other. All students know they are capable of getting an "A" if they complete an assignment. This can create a classroom atmosphere of collegiality and high expectations for all students.

2. The grading of papers doesn't seem as judgmental. If a teacher beforehand explains to the students what criteria is needed for an "A," "B," "C," "D" or "F," then it is harder for a kid to go home and say he got a "D" because the teacher hates him. The grading will seem more reasonable and fair.

3. If the criteria are sound and based on grade-appropriate standards, criterion-referenced grading can reduce "grade inflation." Grade inflation means that students are given higher grades that they actually should. Reasons for this are many, and some are understandable, although even in those cases it should still not happen. Some teachers inflate grades because "the kid is a good kid." As a teacher it is difficult to give an all-around good student a bad grade. Another reason for grade inflation could be the area in which the school is located. For example, a smaller community or an at-risk community could have a different idea of what it takes to meet a certain academic standard than a neighboring affluent community. The problem with this is that eventually students from both communities will hit the workforce, and although they both think they've learned the same information, the level of rigor they were held to will have an impact on how far they will be able to succeed. Because of all the situations mentioned above, it is crucial that we as educators grade our students based on what the academic standards expect them to know, and the knowledge they have shown to achieve those academic standards.

4. The criteria for grading can be used by the students as a checklist before the work is submitted. Because the students know the criteria, they can refer to it to ensure they are incorporating all aspects into their work. This creates a higher-quality of work from all students. The key to successful criterion-referenced grading is the creation and the successful use of a grading rubric.

Table 10.3. Business Letter Checklist

Key Elements	Yes	No
The letter contains the sender's address.	_____	_____
The letter contains the recipient's name and address.	_____	_____
The month is written out, and the letter includes the day and year in the date.	_____	_____
The first letter of the salutation is capitalized.	_____	_____
A colon is placed after the recipient's name is the salutation.	_____	_____
The first body paragraph clearly explains why the letter is being written.	_____	_____
The letter follows consistent block form.	_____	_____
The closing body paragraph restates the letter's purpose.	_____	_____
Only the first word of the closing is capitalized.	_____	_____
A comma follows the closing.	_____	_____
The business letter has a formal tone.	_____	_____

A scoring rubric is a scoring tool containing criteria and a performance scale that allows us to define and describe the most important components that comprise complex performances and products (Arter and McTighe, 2001). The key to this definition is the last part. Items that comprise of complex performances and products need a tool to ensure the teacher is grading consistently and grading each portion of the performance or product.

A rubric is not a checklist. A checklist only shows if something is included or not included; it's more of a "yes/no" tool than a rubric. A checklist does not provide levels of performance or a rating. For example, Table 10.3 is a checklist for a business letter.

As you can see, in the checklist, there is no degree of success; it is just a matter of either the item being present or not. This is okay for basic tasks, but once the assignment gets more complex, a checklist will no longer suffice.

Rubrics assist in consistency of scoring. Rubrics help the teacher stray from personal judgment and score a paper or performance based on where it falls in the rubric, not the teacher's opinion.

Rubrics can help the teacher and student by clarifying the goal of the product or performance and what targets the student needs to focus on for quality. The rubric explains what qualities differ between a poor assignment and a quality assignment. Because the students know what qualities are expected for an "A" paper, there is a better chance they will include those qualities within their work.

There are two types of rubrics that a teacher can use: a holistic rubric and an analytical trait rubric (Arter and McTighe, 2001). With a *holistic rubric*, all the traits of the scoring rubric are combined to provide one final overall score. With an *analytical trait rubric*, each trait is independently scored and a separate score is given for each trait.

The number of traits in a rubric really doesn't matter. The most important thing is that each trait focuses on an important part of the product or skill, and that trivial items aren't added just for the sake of adding more traits to the rubric. Most rubrics have a scale score ending between four and six. The scale score really doesn't matter either, just as long as there are enough points to adequately distinguish different forms of quality.

A *generic rubric* is a rubric that can be used across various tasks. An example of a generic rubric is shown in Table 10.4.

One problem with this rubric is although it provides a scale, it does not define what is needed for each score. Depending on the assignment and how long the teacher has been teaching the specific group of students, a vague, generic rubric may or may not suffice. In the example below, the student would have to already know what constitutes a score of a "4" or a score of a "5." What's nice about this rubric is it has a "you" section where the student scores themselves before submitting the assignment to the teacher, and then a "teacher" area where the teacher can score it.

Table 10.4.   Generic Rubric

Attribute	You	Teacher
The beginning paragraph evidently tells what I will be discussing	1 2 3 4 5	1 2 3 4 5
All additional paragraphs relate to the topic	1 2 3 4 5	1 2 3 4 5
The length is a minimum of one page long	1 2 3 4 5	1 2 3 4 5
Complete sentences are applied throughout the essay	1 2 3 4 5	1 2 3 4 5
Sentences differ in length	1 2 3 4 5	1 2 3 4 5
All sentences do not start with the identical words	1 2 3 4 5	1 2 3 4 5
All sentences are comprehendible	1 2 3 4 5	1 2 3 4 5
Descriptive words are used	1 2 3 4 5	1 2 3 4 5
Slang words are not utilized in the essay, unless used in dialog	1 2 3 4 5	1 2 3 4 5
Overused, cliché words have been replaced with more interesting words	1 2 3 4 5	1 2 3 4 5

A more thorough generic rubric would look like Table 10.5.

In this example, each score point is specifically spelled out. This prevents the teacher from using his judgment and keeps the teacher scoring the paper objectively. This would be considered a generic rubric because it could be used for any type of writing assignment.

Table 10.5. Thorough Generic Rubric

	4	*3*	*2*	*1*
Content	Contains numerous relevant facts and details; assignment requirements for specific content choices are thoroughly met	Contains adequate facts and details to complete the assignment, content choice is met but limited	Some facts and details are present; although some are also missing. Not all content choices are within the assignment.	Facts and details are missing; Content choices do not reflect the assignment
Organization	Includes catchy introduction; logically sequenced paragraphs and contains transitions; strong conclusion which reiterates the main point	Contains an introduction; adequately developed paragraphs and a couple clear transitions; conclusion is present	Logical organization; introduction and conclusion not fully developed; transitions missing	Poor organization; facts and details are stated without paragraphs or transitions; introduction and conclusion are missing
Construction	Sentence construction is varied; spelling and punctuation are correct; sentences flow seamlessly	A few examples of varied sentence construction; few errors in spelling and punctuation; sentences flow, although some choppy sentences are present.	Repetitive sentence construction; some spelling and punctuation errors distract the reader; choppy sentences distract the reader.	Sentence construction errors are present, many spelling and punctuation distract the reader and make the writing impossible to finish

Table 10.6.　Task Specific Rubric

	3	2	1
In tune	All strings are in tune following the EADGBE standard tuning.	Most of the strings are in tune following the EADGBE standard tuning	None of the strings are in tune and don't follow the EADGBE standard tuning.
Nut/Pegs	All six strings are correctly placed on the nut and correctly wound in the peg.	Most of the six strings are correctly placed on the nut and are adequately wound in the peg.	None of the six strings are correctly placed on the nut or correctly wound in the peg.

A *task-specific rubric* lives up to its name; it can only be used for one specific task. For example the follow rubric could be used for tuning a guitar, but probably not much else (it couldn't be used for tuning a piano or other instrument).

In this example the rubric really can't be used for anything but tuning a guitar. It can't even be used for other instruments, like a cello. Because of this, it would be considered a task-specific rubric.

In conclusion, no matter what type of rubric is used, the purpose of a rubric is to help the teacher stray from personal judgment as well as notify the student as to what the expectations are for the assignment. The rubric explains what qualities differ between a poor assignment and a quality assignment.

REFLECTION SCENARIO

Mr. Smith is teaching a 40-minute introductory lesson on the parts of a plant cell. He has gone over the diagram of the plant cell on the board with the students, and he has had them draw, label the parts of the cell, and write the functions of each part of the cell in their science journals. He asks them to close their journals and points to parts of the cell diagram on the board and asks who knows what the name of this part is and what function it serves. Students raise their hands and he calls on one student at a time to name the part and the function until all the parts have been named. There are 35 students in the class. He then moves on to cell reproduction. How will he know that all of his students have learned the parts of the cell and functions before he moves on to the next concept? How would you assess the students for learning?

Think about the last lesson you taught. How did you assess for learning? Is there anything you might want to change about your assessment strategies? How did you know when the students were ready to move on to the next concept?

Chapter 11

Struggling Students

What Is RTI, and What Does It Have to Do with My Teaching?

Humility and knowledge in poor clothes excel pride and ignorance in costly attire.

—William Penn

RTI, or Response to Intervention, is a set of processes for organizing decision making for data-driven instructional practices (Hall, 2008). RTI is based on the beliefs that preventative, early interaction is needed before students fail or need remediation; the use of universal screenings prevent students from "falling through the cracks," and tiered approaches can meet the needs of all students. In its truest model, RTI is basically a problem-solving process in which teachers use data to make decisions about student success and decide which interventions have been used and what outcomes resulted.

The principle of RTI is to assist students as soon as they need it. Before RTI, some students would fall so far behind in school before anyone intervened, and sometimes that intervention would make the student qualify for special education services. As we all know, the label of "special ed" doesn't have positive connotations among students and can have negative effects on a student's morale or enjoyment of school.

What RTI tries to do is identify academic or behavioral concern in students as soon as they occur so the majority of the students can catch up quickly get back into the curriculum they are supposed to be in. This also assists in making sure special education services are truly used for those students that need that type of intervention. Why the need to intervene early in a child's education career? Research shows that it takes four times as long to intervene in fourth grade as in late kindergarten to improve a student's skills by the same amount (Lyon, 1997).

RTI is a school-based or district-based effort. Never will a successful RTI program be based out of only one or two classrooms with no school or district support. The success of RTI truly depends on a reliable assessment tool that can identify students at risk and in need intervention instruction.

Per RTI expert Susan L Hall, there are eight core principals of RTI:

1. We can effectively teach all children
2. Intervene early
3. Use a multi-tier model of service delivery
4. Use a problem-solving model to make decisions within a multi-tier model
5. Use scientific, research-based validated intervention and instruction to the extent available
6. Monitor student progress to inform instruction
7. Use data to make decisions. A data-based decision regarding student response to intervention is central to RTI practices.
8. Use assessment for screening, diagnostics, and progress monitoring

For RTI to truly work, it needs to be a joint effort between general education, special education, Title I, and ELL staff. It is not just a SPED education mandate required by law. The teacher's role in RTI is to ensure they are teaching quality, normal classroom instruction, which is called Tier I of the RTI model.

In the RTI model, there are three tiers of intervention. Tier I is basic, normal classroom instruction using a basal-core reading instruction. As in regular teaching, assessments include end of unit tests and the universal screenings. Tier I instruction is the most important part of RTI, and all students should be engaged in this core instruction (Fuchs and Fuchs, 2005). Using the basic teaching strategies, 70 percent to 80 percent of the class should meet benchmark within the Tier I instruction. If more than 20 percent are in II and III, there is a problem with Teir 1 core.

As stated, Tier 1 is the most important tier, and teamwork is essential. Teachers need to share expertise with colleagues to glean information from those having success with the core instruction and to share strategies with struggling colleagues to help them adjust instruction. The implementation of good Tier I instruction takes time and needs a good core program.

Classroom teachers are the reason if the core is taught successfully or not. Make the most of the core instruction by including a mix of whole- and small-group instruction in which all students participate. Use the differentiation techniques discussed in earlier chapters to attend to individual student needs. Make sure struggling students are seated closer to the teacher, and make sure all students have practice opportunities.

Data is another key part of quality Tier I instruction. Review data often to assess how students are doing, and differentiate and change instruction as needed.

For the students who do not meet benchmark in Tier I, they are then moved to the Tier II interventions. These interventions are only for the students who did not meet benchmark and the interventions should only be used short term. In this tier, students are grouped by their deficits. Using direct instruction, the teacher works with the students on the specific deficits. In Tier II, all activities need to be teacher directed.

For the students who still struggle in Tier II, RTI has a final tier, Tier III. As stated above, Tier II is to be used short term. Students who still need more time can be placed in Tier III, in which the focus is very intense. As Susan Hall states, "In Tier III the curriculum consists of a program in which the skills are arranged in a sequence—all skills are taught rather than just a few. Teachers use more modeling to show the task, and more scaffolding is provided" (Hall, 2008). The time allotted in Tier III should be double the time allotted in Tier II, allowing for more repetition and specific teacher feedback.

TUTORING—A SOMETIMES FORGOTTEN WAY TO HELP STRUGGLING STUDENTS

Year in and year out, dreaded math and language exams stand as the supreme fear of many American students who aren't testing at grade level. By the 12th grade, 23 percent of students remain below basic reading level, and that figure does not include those who dropped out due to poor literary skills (Potter, 1999). With state and national exams requiring all students to perform at a high level, and tests built on knowledge that they don't possess, many students in years past have given up on their educational dreams.

This is where the importance of tutoring comes into play. Research has indicated that tutoring works. A meta-analysis of 65 published studies on tutoring discovered positive achievement effects across all of the studies (Cohen, Kulik, and Kulik, 1982). Tutoring students today can help prevent many of the social ills that could appear in the future. Dropouts are three times more likely to be unemployed than high school graduates. Also, almost one-half of the U.S. prison population in 1992 were high school dropouts (Ainsworth, 1995).

Tutoring has two main benefits: its ability to adapt to the individual learner's needs, and also the emotional benefits of the one-on-one relationship (Potter, 1999). Through tutoring, the instruction can be conveyed at the student's individual pace or learning style. The tutor can modify learning cues based on one student's response, and simple misunderstandings can be discovered without delay. Tutoring is also emotionally stabilizing in that there is no competition from faster learners. Through brain research, we now know that a student's emotional state strongly affects their learning. Due to this, it is important that the tutor provide a home atmosphere and classroom environment to provide a positive experience (Shoemaker and Eklund, 1989). In addition, shy or insecure children may find it easier to risk making a mistake in a one-on-one environment.

The concept of peer tutoring has also shown great promises in the classroom. Because children are learning from their peers, they tend to use a similar language, and both parties generally feel more open to expressing their ideas and concerns (Kalkowski, 1995). Research on peer tutoring points out that the intervention is relatively efficient in improving both tutees' and tutors' scholastic and social development (Swengel, 1991).

Finally, students also need to feel that tutoring is an opportunity, not a punishment (Schneider, 2000). If student perceive tutoring as a chance to improve themselves, not only will they walk away with extra knowledge of their core classes, but they'll also walk away with improved self-worth and poise that has a more lasting value.

REFLECTION SCENARIO

The Leadership Team of the school has asked their data coach and math department to sift and sort students according to first quarter benchmark assessments in Algebra I in order to tier instruction. Most of the students fall into Tier III, and Tier II has more students than Tier 1. What are some strategies that the math department might try to fill in the gaps for their students in the most efficient ways possible? What does RTI look like at your school and describe your role(s) in tiered instruction?

Chapter 12

The Role of "Coaching" in Education and Why Teachers Need to Be Open to It

The beginning of knowledge is the discovery of something we do not understand.

—Frank Herbert

Michael Jordan and Tiger Woods, although on top of their profession, employ coaches to improve their success rate. Professional development is an important concept in educational success. Unfortunately, whether the professional development opportunity is a one-day workshop or an academy offered over several months, the practices and strategies are not likely to be implemented without accountability or coaching.

Good teachers and administrators always strive for improvement. Different studies show that educators are more likely to implement new strategies when they have coaching and feedback accompanying their professional development. Teachers and administrators whose professional development includes coaching are more likely to apply new ideas and concepts in their practice (Neufeld, and Roper, 2003).

In his book, *Masterful Coaching*, Robert Hargrove uses this definition of a coach:

A coach is someone who (1) sees what others may not see through the high quality of his or her attention or listening, (2) is in the position to step back (or invite participants to step back) from the situation so that they have enough distance from it to get some perspective, (3) helps people see the difference between their intentions and their thinking or actions, and (4) helps people cut through patterns of illusion and self-deception caused by defensive thinking and behavior.

Recently published descriptions (Anderson, and Anderson, 2004; Poglinco, Bach, Hovde, Rosenblum, Saunders, and Supovitz, 2003) show coaches fulfill a wide range of roles, including the following:

- Help teachers implement new curricular programs
- Consult with and mentor teachers and administrators
- Support educators as they embed knowledge, skills, and techniques into their daily practice
- Plan and research
- Lead discussion groups
- Facilitate study or book groups

Other studies (Bloom, Castagna, Moir, and Warren, 2005) conclude that basic skills associated with most successful coaching programs in education include:

- trust building
- listening
- observing
- questioning
- giving feedback

Current research points to coaching as a successful way to increase teacher and student achievement. This research has found that teachers who work with coaches demonstrated an unambiguous understanding of the purposes and uses of the new strategies more than teachers who were not coached, and other studies have found coaching increases teacher motivation and decreases burn-out (Joyce and Showers, 2002).

THE BENEFITS OF COACHING

Other reports have found that significant improvements in student achievement materialized only when site-level guidance and support was provided to the teacher (Joyce and Showers, 1995). When training or professional development is accompanied by coaching, the transfer of material into the classroom increases to 80–90 percent, compared to 5–10 percent with coaching.

There are many different definitions and perceptions of academic coaching in education. In order for an academic coach to truly benefit a site, both the administrator and the coach need to understand their goals and responsibilities.

It is important that implementation, accountability, and professional development needs are addressed when a coach is brought into a school or district. The principal and coach should meet to clarify their roles and create a transparent relationship. There are eight strategies that can help administrators and coaches collaborate to bring positive change and increased student academic achievement to their school (Moller and Pankake, 2006):

1) *Collaboratively create a plan and monitor the plan regularly.* Do the administrator and the coach have the same vision? Has a timeline been set with long-term and short-term goals? Has time been set aside to meet regularly?
2) *Discuss roles and relationship.* Has the principal stated her expectations of the coach, and has the coach stated his expectations of the principal? Outlining a clear job description for the coach and making this job description known to the staff can assist in limiting resistance and divisiveness within the staff. The administrator and coach need to have a working relationship, so it is worth the time to discuss when their roles will be the same (observing teachers, analyzing assessments) and when they will differ (evaluation vs. feedback, supervisor vs. peer).
3) *Be available.* Is the principal accessible to the coach for problem solving and discerning the professional needs the staff requires? Coaches are powerless without the action of the principal. The coach must regularly communicate with the principal regarding the needs of the faculty, as well as the successes and challenges being faced.
4) *Provide access to resources.* Does the coach have access to data, materials, and human resources?
5) *Focus on instructional leadership.* Does the role of the coach focus on increasing teacher capacity? The coach should remain an academic asset and not be used for operational tasks such as inventory, discipline or substitute teaching.
6) *Avoid overload.* Are the coach's responsibilities realistic?
7) *Assist the coach's relationship with peers.* Does the instructional staff know exactly what the coach is expected to do and not do? Has the coach been given low-risk tasks to help ease her into the new role? Is the coach given opportunities to share successes with the staff? The role of both the coach and the principal should be explained to the staff as well as what the expectations are for the "coachees." By showing that they are fully behind the coaching protocol, administrators can eliminate some of the resistance the coach might encounter.
8) *Provide development opportunities.* Has professional development been made available to academic coaches to prepare them for the responsibilities of being a coach?

THE COACH'S ROLES AND RESPONSIBILITIES

A concerted effort to define roles and expectations for the new academic coach will position all for success as administrators, coaches, educators, and staff are united in their goal for a culture of learning and increased student academic achievement at their site.

The teacher-coach relationship is truly a relationship, meaning that it takes time to build and trust needs to be a key factor if it is to succeed. One study found that within six weeks of starting a new school year, 85 percent of teachers who worked with instructional coaches implemented at least one new instructional strategy (Deussen, Coskie, Robinson, and Autio, 2007). One can assume that in these successful cases, the coach took the time to identify and acknowledge the teacher's individual strengths, confirm what the teacher was doing correct, connect with the teacher's interests, try to make personal connections with the teacher, and probably asked many questions.

The coach cannot be successful though unless the teacher openly allows them access to the classroom and is willing to listen to what the coach has to say. The teacher needs to know that the coach is there to help, not to evaluate or "tattle" to the principal about the teacher's weaknesses. As stated in the beginning of this chapter, even the best athletes have coaches to help them get better. This should be no different in the classroom. No matter if the teacher has been in the profession for 30 years or 30 minutes, in a culture of learning the focus should be on continuous improvement.

REFLECTION SCENARIO

Mr. M has just come on board as the new instructional coach at XYZ Middle School. He has set up appointments with the staff and Mr. Ruiz's, the 7th Grade ELA teacher's appointment is next Tuesday morning before school begins. Mr. M starts the meeting by sharing his roles and responsibilities as a coach. Mr. M explains that he is there to give feedback to the teachers and assist in helping teachers to move their practices forward. What questions would you have for the new coach? What would you want to know that might help build the trust relationship that research says must exists to foster a successful coaching experience for teachers? Think about the areas of strengths and weaknesses in your own practice. Look back at the coaching strategies in this chapter and describe how a coach might help you to move to the next level in your teaching.

Chapter 13

Essentials in Writing—Another Thing Every Teacher Needs to Know How to Do

I prefer tongue-tied knowledge to ignorant loquacity.

—Marcus Tullius Cicero

We don't know all the answers. If we knew all the answers we'd be bored, wouldn't we? We keep looking, searching, trying to get more knowledge.

—Jack LaLanne

Just as the authors of this book believe that every teacher is a vocabulary teacher, we also believe that every teacher is a writing teacher. It is hard to find a class where a student isn't writing something, and if a student is writing, it is our job as educators to help the student be successful.

The most groundbreaking research on what elements should be included in writing instruction comes from the publication *Writing Next: Effective Strategies to Improve Writing of Adolescents in Middle and High Schools* (Graham and Perin, 2007). This publication provides elements in effective writing instruction, and although it is geared toward middle school and high school, the elements can be adapted for earlier grades as well.

Writing Next identified 11 elements of current writing instruction found to be effective for helping students learn to write well and to use writing as a tool for learning. In this book, we will discuss nine of the elements: writing strategies, summarization, collaborative writing, specific product goals, word processing, sentence combining, prewriting, study of models, and writing for content learning. As stated in earlier chapters of this book, assessment data should be taken into account to specify which element is best suited for a specific class or student. There is not enough time in the school year to randomly try forms of instruction and hope that they will work.

Writing strategies are basically student strategies for preparing, revising, and editing work. Examples are provided at the end of the book. Various studies have shown that the quality of student work increases when teachers previously covered ways to plan, revise, and edit compositions (Bonk and Graham, 2006). Brainstorming, outlining, paragraph shrinking, and peer revising are two forms of writing strategies.

Summarization entails teaching students a system of how to summarize texts, or restating the main ideas in very few words. One example is the use of an index card. A well-written summary should be able to fit in that space. Summarization helps students retain information.

Collaborative writing allows students to work in teams to plan, outline, revise, and edit their compositions. When pairing students, do not let "birds of a feather flock together" by placing the lowest scoring students together (Smith, 2009). As previously stated, it is also imperative that the highest scoring student is not placed with the lowest scoring student. Use this system: if you have 30 kids in the class, rank them by ability. Place student 1 with student 15, 2 with 16 and so on.

Once the partnerships are formed, the students are told to work as partners on a writing task. Throughout the task, the teacher monitors the classroom and assists as necessary while providing specific feedback.

Specific product goals provide students with objectives to focus on particular aspects of their writing. In other words, the teacher assigns students specific, reachable goals for the writing they are to complete. This could focus on a specific writing trait.

Word processing uses computers as instructional supports for writing assignments. Most students have been born and raised with a computer, and in most studies the use of word processors has a consistently positive impact on writing quality.

Sentence combining teaches students to construct more complex and complicated sentences. Sentence combining instruction involves teaching students to construct more sophisticated sentences by combining two or more basic sentences into a single line of information.

Prewriting, like writing strategies, helps students organize their work- in this case before the even start the assignment. Prewriting can include gathering possible information, making a visual representation, group planning, or reading materials and taking notes on the topic they will begin to write about. A template to assist students in prewriting a compare-contrast paper is provided at the end of the book.

Study of models provides students with opportunities to read and analyze good writing. This will also provide the students with an exemplar of what the teacher is looking for in a good paper. When using models, the teacher should explain to students the critical elements, patterns, and forms that create the exemplary piece. When studying models, provide examples of exemplary writing and explain exactly why the writing samples are exemplars. Also, show bad examples of writing and explain what is missing in these samples, as well as what would be needed make these samples exemplary.

Writing for content learning involves students writing in every class, no matter what. As a teacher, you might not have much control in this, but you can educate your peers as to why writing in every class is important. As speaking puts "more miles on the tongue," writing in every class puts more words on the page. The more a student writes, with specific feedback from the teacher, the higher the quality will become.

Based in Arizona, the authors of this book have seen the English Learner population receive much attention when the topic of education is discussed. Nationally, the English Language Learner (ELL) population is one of the largest student subgroup in the country. This group can present difficulties in teaching instruction, but rest assured, the elements stated for writing are also effective with this unique group of learners.

Research tells us that specific examples and opportunities for student engagement benefit ELL students, and the good news is this effective instruction also shows increased academic success for English speakers as well (Echevarria, Vogt, and Short, 2004). Although this book will not go into detail regarding teaching strategies for ELL students, there are a few concepts that every teacher can incorporate in their classrooms to assist ALL students:

- The posting and explaining of clear goals and objectives
- Many opportunities to learn, including redundant information such as gestures, visual cues, and graphic organizers
- Consistent and pre-planned class routines
- Active engagement and participation
- Specific and timely feedback
- Opportunities to discuss and apply new learning, including extra practice and time to grapple with a word or concept
- Interaction with other students, especially those who are language proficient
- regular assessments with re-teaching, especially with comprehension and vocabulary

- Paraphrase students' remarks and encourage expansion
- Target both content and language development in every lesson

REFLECTION SCENARIO

Your writing scores are low, and your team meets to consider strategies to implement school-wide that will help students to organize thoughts and practice summarizing skills. What are some strategies that you might suggest to your colleagues? How would you implement the strategies throughout the school and enlist the help of all content areas?

Chapter 14

Professional Development for Teaching and Learning

> To keep abreast of this new knowledge and understanding, educators at all levels must be continuous learners throughout the entire span of their professional careers.
>
> —Thomas Guskey

As educators, professional development is not only necessary for requirements for continuing certification, but also necessary to stay current in the professional practice that leads to a positive impact ultimately for our students. As in any professional's career, albeit in the business world or in the education arena, professional development plays an important role for those seeking leadership positions or career advancement (Guskey, 2000).

Staff development, in-service, and training are all terms used interchangeably with professional development (Garet, Porter, Desimone, Birman, and Yoon, 2001). One definition by Darling-Hammond and McLauglhin (1996) defines professional development "as deepening teachers' understanding about the teaching and learning process and the students they teach which must begin with pre-service education and continue throughout a teacher's career." Guskey (2000) defines professional development in education as "those processes and activities designed to enhance the professional knowledge, skills, and attitudes of educators so that they in turn, improve the learning of students.".

Professional development should be ongoing and meaningful (Fullen, 1991). Yet, many times professional development ends up being what experts call "One Shot or Drive-by PD" covering random topics that are often unrelated to an educator's professional needs (Coe, Cocoran, David, Kannapel, and McDiarmid, 1997; Darling-Hammond and McLaughlin, 1995;

Guskey, 2000; Sykes, 1996; Sparks, 2002). So as an educator, what can you do to ensure that your professional development will be targeted to your specific needs to improve your professional knowledge that will translate into improvements in your practice and lead to increased academic achievement for the students you teach?

In order for professional development to make a difference, it should not only be continuous, but also needs to be job-embedded, data driven, and targeted to the specific needs of students and staff (Fullen, 1991; Reitzug, 2002; Sparks, 2002). The data-driven component for determining what you as a professional need to move your practice forward is paramount to developing your individual professional development goals and plans. Teacher evaluation systems and informal instructional feedback systems should be in place in your district and school. Possible data points to analyze and inform professional development needs include not only student level data, but observation data from informal walk-throughs, formal evaluations, peer coaching observations, and your own teacher classroom reflection journaling data or observation.

PLANNING FOR YOUR PROFESSIONAL DEVELOPMENT

There are three keys ideas to assist the teacher in planning a successful professional development program:

- First, it is important to have a clear professional goal in mind for yourself and determine what outcomes you will expect as a result of the professional development is seen as necessary for success.
- Second, the goals should be meaningful to you and your practice.
- Finally, decide how you will know you have reached your goal and set benchmarks to gauge your progress along the way. What results do you expect for you and your students? (Guskey, 2000)

Aside from the many university programs (both face-to-face and online) available for graduate courses and degrees that may be a component of a professional development plan, this section discusses state-wide , district or charter-wide, or site-based professional development designs. Delivery methods and platforms for professional development that provide opportunities for new learning have been categorized by several experts into what is known as the seven major models of professional development (Drago-Severson, 1994; Guskey, 2000; Joyce and Showers, 1995; Sparks and Loucks-Horsley, 1989). Table 1 provides a list of the models with the description of how experts define each model.

Table 14.1. Seven Models of Professional Development

The Seven Models of Professional Development

Model	Description
Training	Classic workshop often used to give an overview on a topic or topics to many participants at once
Observation/ Assessment	Administrators observe participants or peers who give feedback on their performance, participants' reflections drive change in practice
Improvement Process	Participants are asked to research, develop, and implement a program to bring about reform
Study Groups	Participants study and work together to solve an identified problem
Inquiry/Action Research	Participants improve their classroom practice by conducting action research
Individually Guided Study	Participant identifies an area of focus for personal growth and selects activities and assessments to foster own learning
Mentoring	Less experience participants are matched with a master educator to develop a mutually beneficial relationship that will lead to a sharing of ideas and growth for both mentor and mentee.

Note: Adapted from Guskey (2000)

Although there will opportunities to be part of a group of administrators or educators that take part in the first four professional development models at some time during your career, the last three models are specifically geared for individual professional development experiences. Inquiry and reflection on one's own practice is often seen as one of the most valuable forms of professional development.

TEACHER ACTION RESEARCH AS PROFESSIONAL DEVELOPMENT

Teacher action research is the reflective systematic process of an educator identifying a problem in his or her practice, and then conducting an inquiry that helps the educator understand more fully the "nature of the problem" (Stringer, 2007). Teacher action research is unique in that in most cases it leads to an understanding of the problem particular to that teacher's classroom practice and leads to action particular to that classroom. Mills (2007) simplifies teacher action research into four steps:

- Identify an area of focus
- Collect data
- Analyze and interpret data
- Develop an action plan

Mills (2007) further emphasized that teacher action research must be a process that the teacher determines to undertake of their own volition and stresses that teacher action research is not something that teachers be directed to do. In any case, this type of professional development is usually selected by unique individuals who are highly committed to continuous improvement and to a culture of learning.

PROFESSIONAL LEARNING COMMUNITIES

Districts and schools that promote a culture of learning encourage a variety of professional development opportunities and provide operational flexibility to ensure planned time and schedules that accommodate educators. One structure that has been shown to be effective for professional development is the professional learning community.

Collaboration has been identified as a key component in professional development and is the foundation of professional learning communities (DuFour, 2004). In recent years the definition of professional learning communities has become blurred and been used in education to signify anything from a book study group to a school department team (DuFour, 2004). Hord defines a professional learning community as "a group of responsible educators who are committed to and share a common purpose of continuous learning. The focus is not only on their own learning but specifically on studying and acquiring whatever it takes to ensure their students are learning" (Hord, 2009). Through professional learning communities, members of the school community can purposefully collaborate to learn and construct meaning together with colleagues (DuFour, 2004; Hord, 2009; Vygotsky, 1978).

Perhaps one of the most important supports leadership can provide for teachers engaged in professional development is that of an effective instructional coach. As stated in the chapter on coaching, research has shown that the likelihood of a teacher effectively implementing the new professional development learning in the classroom increases from 5–10 percent without coaching to 80–95 percent with coaching (Joyce and Showers, 2002). It is important to be open to the mentor instructional coach and build a trusting relationship over time. The expectation of the coach is not only to mentor, but to observe and provide timely and specific feedback to the teachers. Coaches model lessons and may also deliver training and professional development.

One caution needs to be stated clearly at this point. Leadership needs to understand that the coach is there to mentor the teacher, and the coach should not be placed in an evaluative role. It is inappropriate to place the coach in anything other than a coaching relationship with the teachers. One of the most effective skills an instructional coach must have is the ability to develop trusting relationships (Toll, 2005). An effective instructional coach can be a valuable asset to teachers and assist in the implementation of professional development at the practice level.

No matter what model of professional development a teacher chooses the focus should always be teaching and learning with the end result as improved teacher knowledge and skills and increased student academic achievement.

REFLECTION SCENARIO

Think about where you might see yourself in the education profession in the next three years? What is your professional goal? What are your expected outcomes when you achieve your goals? What will this mean for your practice and your students?

Chapter 15

How to Present to Your Peers

This joy of discovery is real, and it is one of our rewards. So too is the approval of our work by our peers.

—Henry Taube

There's a good chance that, at some point, you will be asked to present information to your peers. This could be a large group—for instance, all the math teachers in your district. The authors believe that even when we are teaching our colleagues, we need to model the best practices that we use in the classroom. Anita Archer offers a few points of how to present to a large group of people (Archer, 2007):

NOTES ON PRESENTING TO YOUR PEERS

- Set the tone—do not make participation optional. This is exactly the same as how you teach in the classroom. Participant engagement in staff development equates to the expectation of student engagement when teaching at the classroom level.
- Model each activity with a few lines to help participants understand what is expected.
- Remember the wait time we talked about earlier. This is important for adults as well.
- Model/Think/Pair/Share. Walk the room and write some of the audience responses on an overhead. Share with group. Remember, just because they are adults doesn't mean they can't participate or have to be lectured to.

- Chunk the information parts of the presentation and give plenty of time for processing the information.
- Just as we expect in the classroom, the facilitators or presenters should be the "guide on the side" rather than the "sage on the stage."
- Constantly assess the audience for understanding. Always use both a PowerPoint and an overhead. Use the PowerPoint to talk from, and use the overhead to demonstrate practices. Most school teachers use overheads, so by using one in your presentation you model what they can do. Make sure that the participant responses you write or display on the overhead are accurate and correct. To shield what's coming up on the overhead, put paper under it, not on top of it. That way the presenter can still see what's coming next.
- Have high expectations for your audience. It is a matter of respect.
- Get to know your audience. Show up early and talk to participants if possible to find out what they know (background knowledge), and what they are hoping to get out of the presentation.
- Scaffold the skills that you are presenting. For example, spend plenty of time on phonemic awareness. What is fluency? What is decoding? What is comprehension? Dr. Archer did this to ensure that teachers who may not have been "reading teachers" in the audience had what they needed to understand strategies to address those areas.
- How to handle people who want to all the attention: Look at them as they pose a question, then turn away toward the entire audience. Generalize the question and give an answer to the entire group. If it is a personal question, tell them that you are available during the break or lunch to discuss this one on one with them. Listen to them and never get angry.
- If applicable, make use of participant's name tags and make sure that you call on them by name.
- Engage the audience: use humor and personal stories, but make sure both have a point that ties back to the subject matter.
- Make big points from the same place in the room.
- Wander the room, but stop and stand in one place when talking. Don't walk and talk at the same time. This can be distracting.
- "Teach the stuff, let go of the fluff." Stick to the parts of the presentation that matter and the parts you want the audience to walk away with.
- Model best practices: keep a pace or rhythm in the teaching. Don't go too fast, but make sure you also don't go too slow.

REFLECTION SCENARIO

Think about a time that you attended a professional development in-service or training session. How did the presenter structure the learning? Are there any strategies mentioned in this chapter that the presenter did well? Are there any strategies you would add? Explain the reason why you would choose these specific strategies.

Important Vocabulary Teachers Need to Know

Accountability: Responsibility to someone or for some activity.

Accuracy: The ability to recognize words when they are read.

Achievement Gap: The inequality on a number of educational measures between the performance of groups of students, especially groups defined by gender, race/ethnicity, and socioeconomic status.

Active Engagement: Instructional activities involving students in doing things and thinking about what they are doing.

Active Learning: anything course-related that all students in a class session are called upon to do other than simply watching, listening and taking notes.

Assessment: Methods used to judge the performance of an individual, group or organization.

Automaticity: Acting or done without volition or conscious control; involuntary.

Balanced Assessment System: A variety of assessments are used, for a variety of purposes and communication about results facilitates student involvement and ownership of learning.

Baseline Data: Data collected to establish and understand the existing conditions before any kind of experimental manipulation begins.

Benchmark: A standard for judging a performance.

Check for Understanding: When a teacher gauges what students are getting and what they need to work on more.

Choral Reading: The entire class is reading the same thing at the same time.

Classroom Management: The provisions and procedures necessary to establish and maintain an environment in which instruction and learning can occur.

Cloze Reading: The teacher reads the passage, but occasionally stops on a word and the class is expected to say that word out loud.

Common Formative Assessment: An assessment typically created collaboratively by a team of teachers responsible for the same grade level or course. Common formative assessments are frequently administered throughout the year to identify (1) individual students who need additional time and support for learning, (2) the teaching strategies most effective in helping students acquire the intended knowledge and skills, (3) program concerns—areas in which students generally are having difficulty achieving the intended standard—and (4) improvement goals for individual teachers and the team."

Criteria: A principle or standard by which something may be judged or decided.

Criterion-referenced Grading: Grading in which a student gets scored based on what criteria they complete.

Curriculum: A blend of educational strategies, course content, learning outcomes, educational experiences, assessment, the educational environment and the individual students' learning style, personal timetable and program of work.

Curriculum Alignment: Assuring that the material taught in the school matches the standards and assessments set by the state or district for specific grade levels.

Curriculum Map: A spatial representation of the different components of the curriculum so that the whole picture and the relationships and connections between their components are easily seen.

Curriculum Mapping: The process where each teacher records the content, that is actually taught, how long it is taught and how they are assessed and aligned to academic standards.

Data: Information, especially information organized for analysis or used to reason or make decisions.

Decoding: The reader is able to understand the sounds that match the symbols and can sound out a word.

Diagnostic Assessment: An assessment that occurs at the beginning of the teaching/learning cycle. This type of assessment will provide the teacher with an understanding of the prior knowledge and skills a student brings to a unit, as well as the strengths and specific learning needs of an individual or groups of students in relation to the expectations that will be taught. Diagnostic assessment is conducted prior to and during teaching and learning to determine:

- what existing knowledge, skills, attitudes, interests, and/or needs the student has
- the range of individual differences

- what program plans and/or modifications are required to meet the needs of individuals or groups of students

Differentiation of Instruction: instructional approaches varied and adapted in relation to individual and diverse students.

Direct Instruction: The explicit teaching of a skill-set using teacher-led instruction or demonstrations of the material, rather than exploratory models such as inquiry-based learning.

Dyslexia: A disability that affects the processing of language in reading, writing, spelling and speaking, usually by reading letters backwards.

Evaluation: The process of examining a subject and rating it based on its important features.

Fluency: To do something accurately and fluidly.

Formative Assessment: Evaluation of student learning that aids understanding and development of knowledge, skills and abilities without passing any final judgment (via recorded grade) on the level of learning.

Grade Inflation: When students are given higher grades that they actually should.

Guaranteed and Viable Curriculum: A plan of what the teacher will teach and what the students will learn. The learning is based on an academic standard, can be taught in the time provided, and has explicit and specific objectives for every subject area, grade level, and course.

Individualized Education Program (IEP): A written educational plan that is developed by a team of professionals, educators, and parents concerned with the education of a special needs person.

Imagery: Visually descriptive.

Knowledge: A collection of facts and information acquired through experience or education or (more generally) the theoretical or practical understanding of a subject.

Needs Assessment: A systematic study that incorporates data and opinions from varied sources in order to create, install and evaluate educational and informational products and services.

Norm-referenced Grading: A type of grading that compares a student's performance to the performance of other students within the class.

Outcomes: The intended results of schooling. What students are supposed to know and be able to do.

Pedagogy: The art and language of teaching.

Portfolio: A collection of student work chosen to represent and document a student's progress over a period of time.

Research-based: The use of rigorous, systematic, and objective methodologies to obtain reliable and valid knowledge.

Results: A consequence, effect, or outcome of something

Rubric: An explicit set of criteria used for assessing a particular type of work or performance.

Scaffold: Any of or combination of cognitive and metacognitive tools or strategies used in instruction either by human or computer-based tutors to help learners gain an understanding that would not be possible by the learner alone

School Climate: Multidimensional aspects of a school encompassing both characteristics of the school and perceptions of the school as a place to work and learn.

Sequence of the Curriculum: The order of items taught.

Self-efficacy: A person has confidence that they will be successful.

Silent Reading: When the each student reads the passage to themselves silently.

Skill: The ability to do something.

Standards: A required or agreed level of quality or attainment; the knowledge or skill that the student needs to learn.

Summative Assessment: Assessed work which contributes to the final outcome of a student's grade, such as examinations, essays, dissertations or presentations.

Symbolic Interactions: The action and reaction toward students based on the assumptions about the individual learner's capabilities.

Time on Task: The percentage of time students are engaged in learning.

Wait Time: The time given for students to recall information.

Validity: How well a test measures what it is intended to measure.

Appendix B

Templates

BLANK WORD MAP TEMPLATE

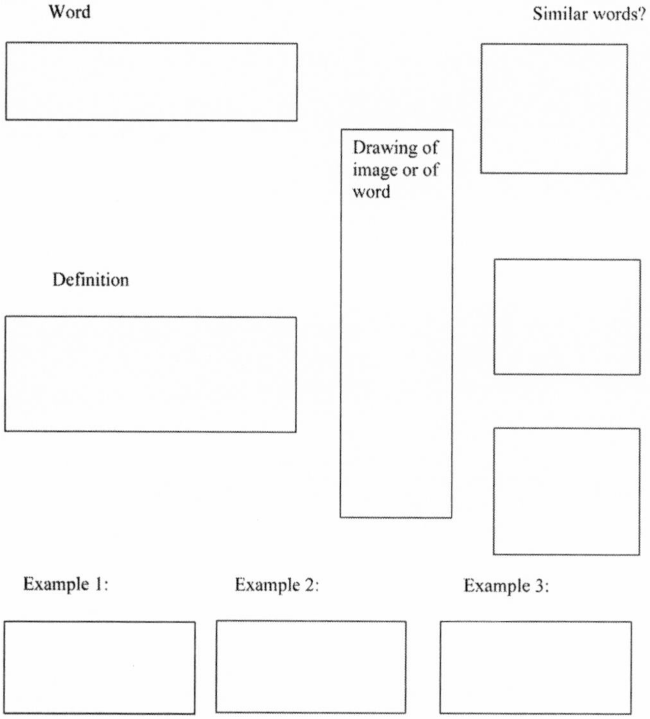

Word

Similar words?

Drawing of image or of word

Definition

Example 1:

Example 2:

Example 3:

Figure B.1

Appendix B

CRITICAL ATTRIBUTES TEMPLATE

Table B.1.

Word and Part of Speech	Critical Attributes	Sentence/Illustration/Examples
	• _____ • _____	
	• _____ • _____ • _____	
	• _____ • _____ • _____	
	• _____ • _____ • _____	
	• _____ • _____ • _____	
	• _____ • _____ • _____	

VOCABULARY TEMPLATE

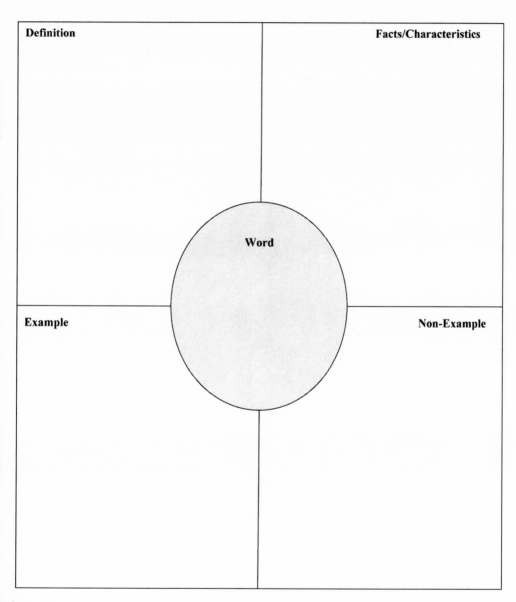

Figure B.2

In this example, a form of imagery is inserted instead of asking for non-examples.

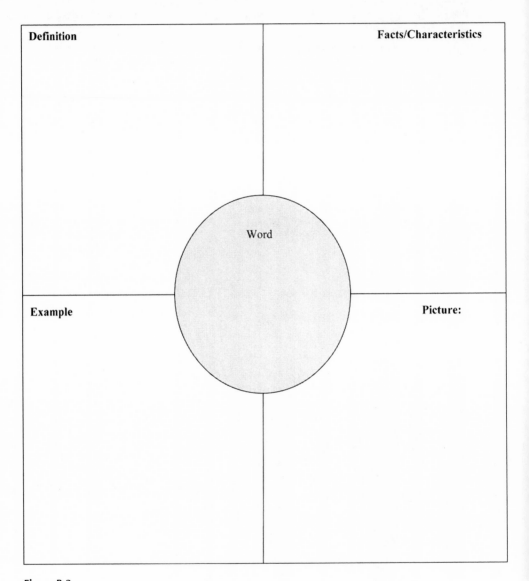

Figure B.3

WORD DIAGRAMS TEMPLATE

Table B.2.

Word	Definition	Similar words or actions	Examples	Non-Examples

SIMILARITIES AND DIFFERENCES TEMPLATE

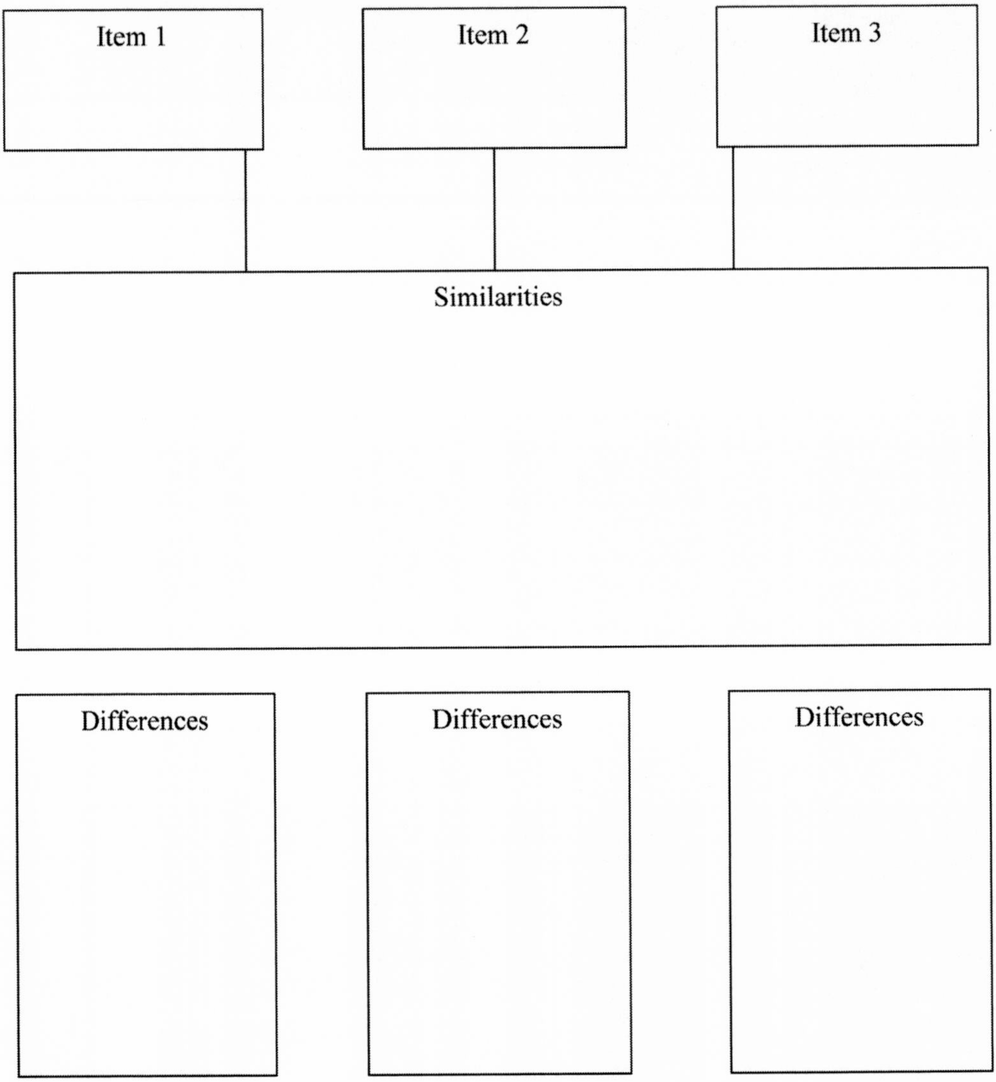

Item 1	Item 2	Item 3

Similarities

Differences	Differences	Differences

Figure B.4

PROS AND CONS TEMPLATE

Table B.3.

Item	Pros	Cons

Bibliography

Ainsworth, R. G. (1995). *Turning potential school dropouts into graduates: The case for school-based one-on-one tutoring.* (Research Report 95–0). Washington, DC: National Commission for Employment Policy.

Akey, T. M. (2006). *School context, student attitudes and behavior, and academic achievement: An exploratory analysis.* New York, NY: MDRC.

Alexander, K. L., Entwisle, D. R., and Dauber, S. L. (1996). Children in motion: School transfers and elementary school performance. *Journal of Educational Research*, 90(1), 3–12. EJ 538 467.

Anderman, L. H., and Midgley, C. (1998). *Motivation and middle school students* [ERIC digest]. Champaign, IL: ERIC Clearinghouse on Elementary and Early Childhood Education.

Anderson, D., and Anderson, M. (2004). *Coaching that counts: Harnessing the power of leadership coaching to deliver strategic value.* Burlington, MA: Elsevier.

Anderson, L., Krathwohl, D., Airasain, P., Cruikshank, K., Mayer, R., Pintrich, O. P., Raths, J., and Wittrock, M. (2001). *A taxonomy for learning, teaching, and assessing.* NY, NY: Addison Wesley, 2001.

Archer, A. (2007). *Competent students, competent teachers.* Paper presented at the Struggling Adolescents conference in Phoenix, AZ.

Archer, A., and Hughes, C. (2011). *Explicit instruction: Effective and efficient teaching.* New York, NY: Guilford.

Arizona Department of Education (2005). *Standards and rubrics for school improvement* (2005 Revised Edition). Phoenix, AZ.

Armstrong, D. G., Henson, K. T., and Savage, T. (2005). *Teaching today: an introduction to education* (7th ed.). Upper Saddle River, NJ: Pearson Prentice Hall.

Arter, J., and McTighe, J. (2001). *Scoring rubrics in the classroom.* Thousand Oaks, CA: Corwin Press.

Baker, M. L., Sigman, J. N., and Nugent, M. E. (2001). *Truancy reduction: Keeping students in school.* Washington, DC: U.S. Department of Justice.

149

Bamburg, J. (1994). *Raising expectations to improve student learning.* Oak Brook, IL: North Central Regional Educational Laboratory.

Bandura, A. (1997). *Self-efficacy: The exercise of control.* New York: W. H. Freeman.

Beck, I. L., McKeown, M. G., and Kucan, L. (2003). Taking delight in words: Using oral language to build young children's vocabularies. *American Educator,* 27(1).

Belland, B., Glazewski, K, and Richardson, J. (2008). A scaffolding framework to support the construction of evidence-based arguments among middle school students. *Education Tech Research Dev.,* 56, 401–22.

Berla, N., Henderson, A. T., and Kerewsky, W. (1989). *The middle school years: A parent's handbook.* Columbia, MD: National Committee for Citizens in Education.

Bernhardt, V. (2004). *Data analysis for continuous school improvement* (2nd ed.). Larchmont, NY: Eye on Education.

Black, P. J., and Wiliam, D. (1998). Inside the black box. Raising standards through classroom assessment. *Phi Delta Kappan,* 80, 139–48.

Blank, W. E. (1997). Authentic instruction. In W. E. Blank and S. Harwell (Eds.), *Promising practices for connecting high school to the real world,* 15–21. Tampa, FL: University of South Florida.

Bloom, G., Castagna, C., Moir, E., and Warren, B. (2005). *Blended coaching: Skills and strategies to support principal development.* Thousand Oaks, CA: Corwin Press.

Bond, Linda A. (1996). Norm- and criterion-referenced testing. *Practical Assessment, Research and Evaluation,* 5(2).

Bonk, C. J., and Graham, C. R. (2006). *Handbook of blended learning: Global perspectives, local designs.* San Francisco, CA: Pfeiffer Publishing.

Bonus, M., and Riordan, L. (1998). *Increasing student on-task behavior through the use of specific seating arrangements.* Unpublished master's thesis. Chicago, IL: Saint Xavier University (ERIC Document Reproduction Service No. ED 422 129).

Bonwell, C. C., and Eison, J. A. (1991). *Active learning: Creating excitement in the classroom.* Washington, DC: ASHE-ERIC Higher Education Report No. 1.

Brewster, C., and Fager, J. (2000). Increasing student engagement and motivation: From *Time-on-task to homework.* Portland, OR: Northwest Regional Educational Laboratory.

Brooks, S. R., Freiburger, S. M., and Grotheer, D. R. (1998). *Improving elementary student engagement in the learning process through integrated thematic instruction.* Unpublished master's thesis. Chicago, IL: Saint Xavier University.

Brookhart, M. S. (2010). *How to assess higher-order thinking skills in your classroom.* Alexandria, VA: Association of Supervision and Curriculum Development.

Capman, C., and King, R. (2003). *Differentiated instructional strategies for reading in the content areas.* Thousand Oaks, CA: Corwin Press, Inc.

Chall, J. S. (1983). *Stages of reading development.* New York, NY: McGraw-Hill.

Chall, J. S., Jacobs, V. A., and Baldwin, L. E. (1990). *The reading crisis: Why poor children fall behind.* Cambridge, MA: Harvard University Press.

Chang, Y. S., Labovitz, G., and Rosansky, V. (1992). *Making quality work: A leadership guide for the results-driven manager.* Essex Junction, VT: Omneo.

Chapman, E. (2003). Alternative approaches to assessing student engagement rates. *Practical Assessment, Research and Evaluation,* 8(13).

Christen, W. L., and Murphy T. J. (1991). Increasing comprehension by activating prior knowledge. *ERIC Digest.* Bloomington, IN: ERIC Clearinghouse on Reading, English, and Communication.

Christle, C. A., Jolivette, K., and Nelson, C. M. (January 1, 2007). School characteristics related to high school dropout rates. *Remedial and Special Education,* 28(6), 325–39.

Cohen, P. A., Kulik, J. A., and Kulik, C. L. C. (1982). Educational outcomes of tutoring: A meta-analysis of findings. *American Educational Research Journal,* 19, 237–48.

Conrad, D. (2005). Building and maintaining community in cohort based online learning. *Journal of Distance Education,* 20(1), 1–20.

Cotton, K. (1989). *Classroom Questioning. Close Up #5.* Portland, OR: Northwest Regional Educational Laboratory.

Cotton, K. (2001). *Expectations and student outcomes.* Retrieved from www.nwrel.org/scpd/sirs/4/cu7.html.

Cunningham, A. E., and Stanovich, K. E. (1997). Early reading acquisition and its relation to reading experience and ability 10 years later. *Developmental Psychology,* 33, 934–45.

Darling-Hammond, L., and McLaughlin, M. W. (1995). Policies that support professional development in an era of reform. *Phi Delta Kappan,* 76(8), 597–604.

Darling-Hammond, L. (1996). *The role of teacher expertise and experience in students' opportunity to learn. Strategies for linking school finance and students' opportunity to learn.* Washington, DC: National Governors Association.

Darling-Hammond, L. (2000). How teacher education matters. *Journal of Teacher Education,* 51, 166–73.

Darling-Hammond, L., Berry, B., and Thoreson, A. (2001). Does teacher certification matter? Evaluating the evidence. *Educational Evaluation and Policy Analysis,* 23, 57–77.

Davis, S. J., and Winek, J. (1989). Improving expository writing by increasing background knowledge. *Journal of Reading,* December.

Deci, E. L., Vallerand, R. J., Pelletier, L. G., and Ryan, R. M. (1991). Motivation and education: The self-determination perspective. *Educational Psychologist,* 26(3–4), 325–46.

Deussen, T., Coskie, T., Robinson, L., and Autio, E. (2007). *Coach can mean many things: Five categories of literacy coaches in Reading First.* Washington, DC: U.S. Department of Education, Institute of Education Sciences, National Center for Education Evaluation and Regional Assistance, Regional Educational Laboratory Northwest.

Dev, P. C. (1997). *Intrinsic motivation and academic achievement: What does their relationship imply for the classroom teacher?* Remedial and Special Education, 18(1), 12–19.

Dochy, F. J. R. C., Segers, M., and Buehl, M. M. (1999). The relation between assessment practices and outcomes of studies: The case of research on prior knowledge. *Review of Educational Research*, 69(2).

Drago-Severson, E. E. (1994). *What does staff development develop? How the staff development literature conceives adult growth.* Unpublished qualifying paper, Harvard University.

Droop, M., and Verhoeven, L. (2003). Language proficiency and reading ability in first and second language learners. *Reading Research Quarterly*, 38(1).

Dropouts and crime. www.schoollibraryjournal.com/article/CA6590701.html.

Drucker, P. (1992). *Managing for the future: The 1990s and beyond.* New York: Truman Talley Books.

DuFour, R. (2004). What is a "professional learning community?" *Educational Leadership*, 61(8), 6.

Dulewicz, V., Malcolm Higgs, M., Mark Slaski, M. (2003). Measuring emotional intelligence: content, construct and criterion-related validity, *Journal of Managerial Psychology*, Vol. 18 Iss: 5, 405–20.

Dunn, M., Bonner, B. and Huske, L. (2007). *Developing a systems process for improving instruction in vocabulary: Lessons learned.* Alexandria, VA: Association of Supervision and Curriculum Development.

Echevarria, J., Vogt, M. E., and Short, D. (2004). *Making content comprehensible for English language learners: The SIOP model*, second edition. Boston, MA: Allyn and Bacon.

Eislzer, C. F. (1983). Perceptual preferences as an aspect of adolescent learning styles. *Education,* 103(3), 231–42.

Ellis, N. and Beaton, A. (1993). Factors affecting the learning of foreign language vocabulary: Imagery keyword mediators and phonological short-term memory. *The Quarterly Journal of Experimental Psychology*, 46A (3), 533–58.

Epstein, J. L. (1987). Toward a theory of family-school connections: Teacher practices and parent involvement. In K. Hurrelman, F. Kaufmann, and F. Losel (Eds.), *Social intervention: Potential and constraints,* 121–36. New York, NY: Aldine.

Evertson, C. M., and Harris, A. H. (1992). What we know about managing classrooms. *Educational Leadership*, 49(7), 74–78.

Evertson, C., and Poole, I. (2006). *Effective room arrangement.* Peabody College/ Vanderbilt University Iris Center.

Evertson, C. M., Emmer, E. T., and Worsham, M. E. (2003). *Classroom management for elementary teachers*, 6th ed. Boston, MA: Allyn and Bacon.

Fay, D., and Cutler, A. (1977). Malapropisms and the structure of the mental lexicon. *Linguistic Inquiry*, 8, 505–520.

Ferguson, R. F., and Womack, S. T. (1993). The impact of subject matter and education coursework on teaching performance. *Journal of Teacher Education*, 44(1), 55–63.

Felch, J., Song, J., and Smith, D. (2010). Who's teaching L.A.'s kids? August 14, 2010, *Los Angeles Times*.

Fetler, M. (1999). High school staff characteristics and mathematics test results. *Education Policy Analysis Archives*, 7(9).

Finn, J. D. (1989). Withdrawing from school. *Review of Educational Research*, 59, 117–42.

Fitterer, H., Harwood, S., Locklear, K., Wright, K., Fleming, P., and Levinsohn, J. (2004). *T4S Classroom observation protocol*. Phoenix, AZ: West Ed.

Fong, A. B., Bae, S., and Huang, M. (2010). Patterns of student mobility among English language learner students in Arizona public schools. In *Issues and Answers Report, REL 2010–No. 093*. Washington, DC: U.S. Department of Education, Institute of Education Sciences, National Center for Education Evaluation and Regional Assistance, Regional Educational Laboratory West. Retrieved from ies.ed.gov/ncee/edlabs.

Forster, M., and Masters, G. (2004). Bridging the conceptual gap between classroom assessment and system accountability. In M. Wilson (ed.), *Towards coherence between classroom assessment and accountability: The 103rd yearbook of the National Society for the Study of Education, Part II* (pp.51–73). Chicago, IL: The University of Chicago Press.

Fuchs, D., and Fuchs, L. S. (2005). Responsiveness-to-intervention: A blueprint for practitioners, policymakers, and parents. In *Teaching Exceptional Children*, 38, 57–61.

Fullen, M. G. (1991). *The new meaning of educational change*. New York, NY: Teachers College Press.

Garan, E. M., and DeVoogd, G. (2008). The benefits of sustained silent reading: Scientific research and common sense converge. *The Reading Teacher*, 62(4), 336–44.

Gardner, H., and Hatch, T. (1989). Multiple intelligences go to school: Educational implications of the theory of multiple intelligences. *Educational Researcher*, 18(8), 4–9.

Garet, M., Porter, A., Desimone, L., Birman, B., and Yoon, K. (2001) What makes professional development effective? Results from a national sample of teachers. *American Educational Research Journal*, 38(4), 915–45.

Gonder, P. (1991). Caught in the middle: How to unleash the potential of average students. Arlington, VA: American Association of School Administrators, 1991. 27 pages. ED 358 554.

Good, T. L. (1987). Two decades of research on teacher expectations: Findings and future directions. *Journal of Teacher Education*, 38(4), 32–47. EJ 358 702.

Gottfredson, G., and Gottfredson, D. (2002). Quality of school-based prevention programs: Results from a national survey. *Journal of Research in Crime and Delinquency*. 39: 3–35.

Graham, S., and Perin, D. (2007). *Writing next: Effective strategies to improve writing of adolescents in middle and high schools—A report to Carnegie Corporation of New York*. Washington, DC: Alliance for Excellent Education.

Green, M. F. (1989). *Minorities on campus: A handbook for enriching diversity.* Washington, DC: American Council on Education.

Guide to using data in school improvement efforts: A compilation of knowledge from data retreats and data use at learning point associates (2004). Naperville, IL: Learning Point Associates.

Guskey, T. R. (2000). Grading policies that work against standards . . . and how to fix them. *NASSP Bulletin*, 84(620), 20–29.

Guskey, T. R. (1982). The effects of change in instructional effectiveness on the relationship of teacher expectations and student achievement. *Journal of Educational Research* 75 (1982): 345–49.

Guskey, T. R. (2000). *Evaluating professional development*. Thousand Oaks, CA: Corwin Press, Inc.

Guskey, Thomas R. (2003). How Classroom Assessments Improve Learning. *Educational Leadership* 60(5) 6–11.

Guthrie, J. T. and Humenick, N. M. (2004). Motivating students to read: Evidence for classroom practices that increase reading motivation and achievement. In P. McCardle and V. Chhabra. (Eds.) *The voice of evidence in reading research* (pp. 329–54). Baltimore, MD: Brookes Publishing.

Haberman, M. (1995). Selecting "star" teachers for children and youth in urban poverty. *Phi Delta Kappan*, Vol. 76, 1995.

Hall, P., and Simeral, A. (2008). *Building teachers' capacity for success: A collaborative approach for coaches and school leaders*. Alexandria, VA: Association for Supervision and Curriculum Development.

Hall, R. M., and Sandler, B. R. (1982). *The classroom climate: A chilly one for women?* Washington, DC: Association of American Colleges.

Hall, S. L. (2008). *Implementing response to intervention: A principal's guide*. Thousand Oaks, CA: Corwin Press.

Hanushek, E. (1971). Teacher characteristics and gains in student achievement: Estimation using micro data. *American Economic Review* 60(2), 280–88.

Hargrove, R. (2003). *Masterful coaching*. San Francisco, CA: Jossey-Bass.

Harris, K. M., Udry, J. R., Muller, C; and Reyes, P. (2010). *National longitudinal study of adolescent health, 1994–2008*: Chapel Hill, NC: Education Data.

Hart, B., and Risley, R. T. (1995). *Meaningful differences in the everyday experience of young American children*. Baltimore, MD: Paul H. Brookes.

Hatzivassiloglou, V., and McKeown, K. (1993). *Towards the automatic identification of adjectival scales: Clustering adjectives according to meaning*. ACL 172–82.

Hawk, P., Coble, C. R., and Swanson, M. (1985). Certification: It does matter. *Journal of Teacher Education*, 36(3): 13–15.

Heacox, D. (2002). *Differentiating instruction in the regular classroom: How to reach and teach all learners, grades 3–12* Minneapolis, MN: Free Spirit.

Heller, R., Calderon, S., and Medrich, E. (2003). *Academic achievement in the middle grades: What does research tell us? A review of the literature*. Atlanta, GA: Southern Regional Education Board.

Heritage, M. (2010). *Formative assessment and next-generation assessment systems: are we losing an opportunity?* The Council of Chief State School Officers (CCSSO).

Heritage, M. (2010). *Formative Assessment: Making it happen in the classroom.* Thousand Oaks, CA: Corwin Press.

Heritage, M., Kim, J., Vendlinski, T., and Herman, J. (2009). From evidence to action: A seamless process in formative assessment? *Educational Measurement: Issues and Practice,* 28(3), 24–31.

Honzay, A. (1986) More is not necessarily better. *Educational Research Quarterly,* 11 (1986–1987): 2–6.

Hord, S. (2009). Professional learning communities: Educators working together toward a shared purpose-improved student learning. *Journal of Staff Development,* Vol. 30 (1).

Jackson, A. W. and Davis, G. A. (2000). *Turning points 2000: Educating adolescents in the 21st century.* New York, NY: Teachers College Press.

Jesse, D. (1995). *Increasing parental involvement: A key to student achievement. What's noteworthy on learners, learning and schooling.* Denver, CO: McRel, Mid-Continent Regional Educational Laboratory.

Jones, F. (2000). *Tools for teaching: Discipline, instruction, motivation,* Hong Kong: Fred Jones and Associates, Inc.

Jones, F. (2007). *Fred Jones tools for teaching: Discipline, instruction, motivation.* Santa Cruz, CA: Frederic H. Jones and Associates.

Joyce, B. and Showers, B. (1995). *Student achievement through staff development* (2nd ed.). New York, NY: Longman.

Joyce, B., and Showers, B. (2002). *Student achievement through staff development.* Alexandria, VA: Association for Supervision and Curriculum Development.

Joyce, B., Wolf, J., and Calhoun, E. (1993). *The self-renewing school.* Alexandria, VA: Association for Supervision and Curriculum Development.

Kalkowski, P. (1995). Peer and cross-age tutoring; In *School improvement research series; Close-up #18.* Portland, OR: Northwest Regional Educational Laboratory.

Kellough, R. D., and Kellough, N. G. (1999). *Secondary school teaching: A guide to methods and resources; planning for competence.* Upper Saddle River, NJ: Prentice Hill.

Kingore, B. (2006). Tiered instruction: Beginning the process. *Teaching for High Potential,* 5–6. www.nagc.org.

Kushman, J. W., Sieber, C., and Heariold-Kinney, P. (2000). This isn't the place for me: School dropouts. In D. Capuzzi and D. R. Gross (Eds.), *Youth at risk: A prevention resource for counselors, teachers, and parents* (3rd ed., pp. 471–507). Alexandria, VA: American Counseling Association.

Laczko-Kerr, I., and Berliner, D. (2002). The effectiveness of Teach for America and other under-certified teachers on student academic achievement: A case of harmful public policy. *Educational Policy Analysis Archives,* 10(37).

Langer, J. A., and Applebee, A. N. (1987). *How writing shapes thinking.* Urbana, IL: National Council of Teachers of English.

Langer, J. A. (2001). Beating the odds: Teaching middle and high school students to read and write well. *American Educational Research Journal,* 38, 837–80.

Langer, J. A. (1984). Examining background knowledge and text comprehension. *Reading Research Quarterly*, 19(4).

Lee, V. E., and Smith, J. B. (1999). *Social support and achievement for young adolescents in Chicago: The role of school academic press. American Educational Research Journal*, 36, 907–45.

Lipton, L., Wellman, B., and Humbard, C. (2001). *Mentoring matters: A practical guide to learning-focused relationships.* Sherman, CT: Mira Via.

Long, S. A., Winograd, P. N., and Bridget, C. A. (1989). The effects of reader and text characteristics on imagery reported during and after reading. *Reading Research Quarterly*, 24(3).

Lumsden, L. S. (1994). *Student motivation to learn* (ERIC Digest No. 92). Eugene, OR: ERIC Clearinghouse on Educational Management.

Lyon, G. R. (July 10, 1997). *Report on Learning Disabilities Research,* Congressional testimony.

MacNiel, A., and Maclin, V. (2005, July 24). *Building a learning community: The culture and climate of schools.* Retrieved from the Connexions Web site: cnx.org/content/m12922/1.2/.

Mandel, S. M. (1999). *Virtual field trips in the cyberage: A content mapping approach.* Arlington Heights, IL: Sky Light Professional Development.

Marzano, R. J., and Pickering D. J. (2005). *Building academic vocabulary: Teacher's manual.* Alexandria, VA: Association for Supervision and Curriculum Development.

Marzano, R. J. (1992). *A different kind of classroom: Teaching with dimensions of learning.* Alexandria, VA: Association for Supervision and Curriculum Development.

Marzano, R. J., Pickering, D. J., Arredondo, D. E., Blackburn, G. J., Brandt, R. S., and Moffett, C. A. (1992). *Dimensions of learning: Training and implementation manual.* Alexandria, VA: Association for Supervision and Curriculum Development.

Marzano, R., Marzano, J., and Pickering, D. (2003). *Classroom management that works.* Alexandria, VA: Association for Supervision and Curriculum Development.

Marzano, R., Walters, T., and McNulty, B. (2005). *School leadership that works.* Alexandria, VA: Association for Supervision and Curriculum Development.

Marzano, R. J. (2004). *Building background knowledge for academic achievement: Research on what works in schools.* Alexandria, VA: Association for Supervision and Curriculum Development.

Mastropieri, M., and Scruggs, T. (2000). *The inclusive classroom: Strategies for effective instruction.* Columbus, OH: Merrill.

Mather, N., and Goldstein, S. (2001). Behavior modification in the classroom. In *Learning disabilities and challenging behaviors: A guide to intervention and classroom management*, (96–117). Arlington, VA: LD Online.

McCarthy, J., and Still, S. (1993). Hollibrook Accelerated Elementary School. In J. Murphy and P. Hallinger (Eds.), *Restructuring schooling: Learning from ongoing efforts,* 63–83. Newbury Park, CA: Corwin.

McCombs, B. L., and Pope, J. E. (1994). *Motivating hard to reach students.* Washington, DC: American Psychological Association.

McDiarmid, G. W., David, J. L., Kannapel, P. K., Corcoran, T. B., and Coe, P. (1997).

Professional development under KERA: Meeting the challenge. Preliminary research. findings prepared for The Partnership for Kentucky Schools and The Pritchard Committee for Academic Excellence.

McKeachie, W.; Pintrich, P.; Yi-Guang, L.; and Smith, D. (1986). *Teaching and learning in the college classroom: A review of the research literature.* Ann Arbor, MI: The Regents of the University of Michigan.

McKenna, M. C., Kear, D. J., and Ellsworth, R. A. (1995). Children's attitudes toward reading: A national survey. *Reading Research Quarterly,* 30, 934–56.

McMillan, J. H. (2000). *Classroom assessment: Principles and practice for effective instruction.* Newark, DE: Pearson Technology Group.

Meier, D. (2000). *The accelerated learning handbook: a creative guide to designing and delivering faster, more effective training programs.* New York, NY: McGraw-Hill Professional.

Moir, E. (1999). The stages of a teacher's first year. In M. Scherer (Ed.). *A better beginning: Supporting and mentoring new teachers.* Larchmont, NY: Eybon Ed.

Moller, G., and Pankake, A. (2006). *Lead with me: A principal's guide to teacher leadership.* Larchmont, NY: Eye on Education.

Murphy J. M., Wehler, C. A., Pagano, M. E., Little, M., Kleinman, R. E., and Jellinek, M. S. (1998). Relationship between hunger and psychosocial functioning in low-income American children. *Journal of the American Academy of Child and Adolescent Psychiatry,* 37.

National Center for Education Statistics. (2005). Integrated postsecondary education data system (IPEDS) fall enrollment survey [Data file]. Washington, DC: U.S. Department of Education.

National Report to Parliament on Indigenous Education and Training, Department of Education, Science and Training (2001). Commonwealth of Australia.

Neufeld, B., and Roper, D. (2003). *Coaching: A strategy for developing instructional capacity—promises and practicalities.* Washington, DC: Aspen Institute Program on Education and the Annenberg Institute for School Reform.

Palincsar, A. S., Brown, A. L., and Campione, J. C. (1993). First grade dialogues for knowledge acquisition and use. In E. A. Forman, N. Minick, and C. A. Stone (Eds.), *Contexts for learning: Sociocultural dynamics in children's development* (pp. 43–57). New York, NY: Oxford University Press.

Pemberton, G. (1988). *On teaching minority students: Problems and strategies.* Brunswick, ME: Bowdoin College, 1988.

Penner, J. G. (1984). *Why many college teachers cannot lecture.* Springfield, IL: Thomas.

Perie, M., Marion, S., and Gong, B. (2009). Moving toward a comprehensive assessment system: A framework for considering interim assessments. *Educational Measurement: Issues and Practice,* 28(3), 5–13.

Pink, D. H. (2011). *Drive: The surprising truth about what motivates us.* Edinburgh, UK: Canongate.

Poglinco, S. M., Bach, A. J., Hovde, K., Rosenblum, S., Saunders, M., and Supovitz, J. A. (2003). *The heart of the matter: The coaching model in America's choice schools.* Philadelphia, PA: University of Pennsylvania, Consortium for Policy Research in Education.

Pollitt, E. (1991). Effects of a diet deficient in iron on the growth and development of preschool and school age children. *Food and Nutrition Bulletin,* 13(2), 110–18.

Potter, J. et al. (1999). *So that every child can read . . . America Reads community tutoring partnerships.* Portland, OR: Northwest Regional Educational Laboratory.

Professional development under KERA: Meeting the challenge. Lexington, KY: The Partnership for Kentucky Schools and The Prichard Committee for Academic Excellence.

Ramirez, D., and Douglas, D. (1989). *Language minority parents and the school: Can home-school partnerships increase student success?* Sacramento, CA: California State Dept. of Education.

Reardon, M. (2008). Americans text more than they talk. *NET.* Sept. 22, 2008.

Reiff, J. C. (1992). *Learning styles.* Washington, DC: National Education Association.

Reitzug, U. C. (2002). *Professional development. School reform proposals: The research evidence.* Greenwich, CT: Information Age Pub.

Renzulli, J., and Smith, L. (1978). *Learning styles inventory: A measure of student preference for instructional techniques.* Mansfield Center, CT: Creative Learning Press, Inc.

Reynolds, A. (1992). What is a Competent Beginning Teacher? A Review of the Literature. *Review of Educational Research,* 62, 1–35.

Rosenshine, B., and Stevens, R. (1986). Teaching functions, in M. C. Wittrock (Ed.) in *Handbook of research on teaching,* 3rd edition. New York, NY: Macmillan.

Rosenthal, R., and Jacobson, L. (1968). *Pygmalion in the classroom.* New York, NY: Holt, Rinehart and Winston.

Rossmiller, R. A. (1983). Time-on-task: A look at what erodes time for instruction. *NASSP Bulletin* 67: 45–49. Thousand Oaks, CA: Sage Publication.

Rovee-Collier, C. (1995). Time windows in cognitive development. *Developmental Psychology,* 31, 147–69. Nuthall, G. A. (1999).

Ruhl, K. L., Hughes, C., and Schloss, P. (1987). Using the pause procedure to enhance lecture recall. *Teacher Education and Special Education* 10: 14–18.

Rumberger, R. W., and Larson, K. A. (1998). Student mobility and the increased risk of high school dropout. *American Journal of Education,* 107(1), 1–35. EJ 583 043.

Rye, J. (1982). *The cloze procedure and the teaching of reading.* Oxford, UK: Heinemann Educational Books Ltd.

Sanders, W., and Rivers, J. (1996). *Cumulative and residual effects of teachers on future student academic achievement.* Research Progress Report.

Schneider, Elaine Ernst. (2000). *Summer tutoring—Good idea or bad?* Available online: www.lessontutor.com/ees11.html.

Schurr, S. L. (1992). Fine tuning your parent power: Increasing student achievement. *Schools in the Middle,* 2(2), 3–9.

Sergiovanni, T. (2001). *The Principalship: A reflective practice.* 5th ed. San Antonio, TX: Trinity Press.

Shoemaker. (1989) Integrative education. A curriculum for the twenty-first century. *OSSC Bulletin Series.* Eugene, OR: Oregon School Study Council.

Shouse, R. D. (1996). Academic press and sense of community: Conflict, congruence, and implications for student achievement. *Social Psychology of Education,* 1, 47–68.

Skinner, E., and Belmont, M. (1991). *A longitudinal study of motivation in school: Reciprocal effects of teacher behavior and student engagement.* Unpublished manuscript. Rochester, NY: University of Rochester.

Smaldino, S., Lowther, D., and Russell, J. (2007). *Instructional media and technologies for learning,* 9th edition. Englewood Cliffs, NJ: Prentice Hall, Inc.

Smith, F. (2009). *Effective types of active engagement.* Paper presented at the Active Engagement and Effective Teaching Practices—A Bridge from Teaching to Learning Conference, Phoenix, AZ, February 29, 2009.

Smith, F. (2009). *Tips to better lectures, lesson plan notes, and practice.* Paper presented at the Active Engagement and Effective Teaching Practices—A Bridge from Teaching to Learning Conference, Phoenix, AZ, February 29, 2009.

Sparks, D. (2002). *Designing powerful professional development for teachers and principals.* Oxford, OH: National Staff Development Council.

Sparks, D., and Loucks-Horsley, S. (1989). Five models of staff development for teachers. *Journal of Staff Development,* 10(4), 40–57.

Sprick, R., Garrison, M., and Howard, L. (1998). *CHAMPS: A proactive and positive approach to classroom management.* Longmont, CA: Sopris West.

Squire, J. R. (1983). Composing and comprehending: two sides of the same basic process. *Language Arts,* 60, 581–89.

Stanovich, K. E., Cunningham, A. E., and Freeman, D. J. (1984). Intelligence, cognitive skills and early reading progress. *Reading Research Quarterly,* 19, 278–303.

Stiggins, R. J. (2008). *Assessment manifesto: A call for the development of balanced assessment systems.* Portland, OR: ETS Assessment Training Institute.

Stover, D. (2000, June 13). Schools grapple with high student mobility rates. *School Board News,* 11, 1–8.

Strangman, N., and Hall, T. (2004). *Background knowledge.* Wakefield, MA: National Center on Accessing the General Curriculum.

Stronck, D. R. (1980). The educational implications of human individuality. *American Biology Teacher,* 42, 146–51.

Strong, R., Silver, H. F., and Robinson, A. (1995). What do students want? *Educational Leadership,* 53(1), 8–12.

Stronge, J., and Hindman, J. (2003). Hiring the Best Teachers. *Educational Leadership,* 60(8), 48–52.

Swengel, E. M. (1991). Peer tutoring: Back to the roots of peer helping. *The Peer Facilitator Quarterly,* 8(4), 28–32.

Sykes, G. (1996). Reform of and as professional development. *Phi Delta Kappan*, Vol 77, 7.

Tauber, R. T. (1998). *Good or bad, what teachers expect from students they generally get!* ERIC document ED 426 985.

Tileston, D. (2004). *What every teacher should know about learning, memory, and the brain.* Thousand Oaks, CA: Corwin Press.

Toll, C. (2005). *The literacy coach's survival guide: Essential questions and practical answers.* Newark, DE: International Reading Association.

Tomlinson, C. A. (2000). Differentiated instruction: Can it work? *The Education Digest.* 65(5) 25–31.

Tomlinson, C. A., and Eidson, C. C. (2003). Differentiation in practice: A resource guide for differentiating curriculum. Alexandria, VA: Association for Supervision and Curriculum Development.

Tomlinson, C. A., and McTighe, J. (2006). *Integrating differentiated instruction and understanding by design.* Alexandria, VA: Association for Supervision and Curriculum Development.

Tomlinson, C. A. (1999). *The differentiated classroom: responding to the needs of all learners.* Alexandria, VA: Association for Supervision and Curriculum Development.

Tomlinson, C. A. (2003). *Fulfilling the promise of the differentiated classroom: Strategies and tools for responsive teaching.* Alexandria, VA: Association for Supervision and Curriculum Development.

Tyler, R. W. (1950). *Basic principles of curriculum and instruction.* Chicago, IL: University of Chicago Press.

Udelhofen, S. (2005). *Keys to curriculum mapping: strategies and tools to make it work.* Thousand Oaks, CA: Corwin Press.

Verdugo, R. and Schnieder, J. (1999). Quality schools, safe schools: A theoretical and empirical discussion. *Education and Urban Society*, 31(3), 286–308.

Voke, H. (2002). Motivating Students to Learn. *ASCD Infobrief*, 2(28).

Vygotsky, L. (1986). *Thought and language.* Cambridge, MA: The MIT Press.

Vygotsky, L. S., (1978). *Mind in society: The development of higher psychological processes.*

Walker, D. (2004). *What every teacher should know about student motivation.* Thousand Oaks, CA: Corwin Press.

Walker, G., Audette, R., and Algozine, R. (1998). Increasing time on task through total quality education. *ERS Spectrum*, 16 (3), 11–16.

Washington, DC: U.S. Department of Justice, Office of Juvenile Justice and Delinquency Prevention.

Wherry, H. (1996). 1996 NAESP Convention, Washington, DC, March 24, 1996.

Wenglinsky, H. (2000). *How teaching matters: Bringing the classroom back into discussions of teacher quality.* Princeton, NJ: Educational Testing Service.

Wiggins, G. (1998). *Educative assessment: Designing assessments to inform and improve student performance.* San Francisco, CA: Jossey-Bass.

Williams, W. M., Blythe, T., White, N., Li, J., Sternberg, R. J., and Gardner, H. (1996). Practical intelligence for school. New York, NY: HarperCollins College Publishers.

Wong, H., and Wong, R. (1991) *The first days of school: How to be an effective teacher,* Mountain View, CA: Harry Wong Publications.

Woods, E. G. (1995). Reducing the dropout rate. In *School Improvement Research Series (SIRS): Research you can use (Close-up No. 17).* Portland, OR: Northwest Regional Educational Laboratory.

Yazzie-Mintz, E. (2007). *Voices of students on engagement: A report on the 2006 High School Survey of Student Engagement.* Bloomington, IN: Center for Evaluation and Education Policy, Indiana University.

Yelland, N,, and Masters, J. (2007). Rethinking scaffolding in the information age. *Computers and Education,* 48, 362–82.

About the Authors

Oran Tkatchov holds an M.Ed. degree in Educational Leadership. He is a former middle school teacher, high school teacher, charter school director, and provider of professional development and school improvement resources.

Shelly Kraynow Pollnow holds an M.Ed. degree in Curriculum and Instruction and has spent her education career in Arizona. She is pursuing her doctorate from Arizona State University where her topics of interest include effective implementation of professional development at the classroom practice level.

CPSIA information can be obtained at www.ICGtesting.com
Printed in the USA
BVOW011230131111

275950BV00003B/35/P